I0480978

In the loving memory of
my dad, who inspired me to
achieve excellence in the life.

# CONTENTS

Promote change and challenge

Balance the big picture with attention to details

Understand each internal interaction through a customer's eyes

Pitfalls to avoid

References

About the author

# PREFACE

*Time does not change us. It just unfolds us.* – Mark Frisch

This book is about a new abnormal that currently pervades business and society as convulsions such as catastrophic events, technological upheavals, and wild swings in business optimism or business optimism rock them. Only the agile and alert will survive in the evolving situation. They face moving targets as their goals as the ground before them continuously shifts. Yet, information technology provides data and visibility into our environment that should stimulate creativity for rapid problem-solving aided by digital tools.

## Complex made simple with digital

Deep-sea oil drilling and production platforms epitomize complexity, uncertainty, and vulnerability to calamities. They have exposure to the turbulence of rough weather during storms. Failures in their systems culminate in explosions, such as of the BP oil platform in 2010, with catastrophic damage to the surrounding environment.

Oil platforms are labyrinths with many of their subsystems and components invisible to the human eye; their inspection is inevitably imperfect, and the pre-emptive correction of faults in them daunting.

Digital twins, however, greatly simplify the control of complex systems such as oil platforms. Shell is one of the energy companies that has adopted an advanced version of digital twin used for product development, remote monitoring of operations, and decision-making simulations.

Each of the processes and systems of an oil platform has virtual images that collectively help visualize it in its entirety, including workflows end-to-end. They are integrated with the Internet of Things (IoT) and receive data on every component's state-of-health in real-time, fed into models to predict breakdowns and find opportunities for pre-emptive maintenance.

At the stage of designing platforms, engineers attempt to resolve the issues with them. Simulations with data help spot lurking vulnerabilities that could come to the surface during times of stress. In subsequent iterations of oil platforms, engineers consider the historical operational experience to make them sturdier. Digital Twins have built-in remote controls for operation managers to make course corrections when they detect anomalies in the data.

Digital transformation is a foundational technology for complex agile systems. Data and analytics create situational awareness that prepares organizations to take action before they are struck by disasters. Understanding the vulnerabilities of their systems helps them fortify them against weather external shocks and catastrophic events. Remote controls allow you to react before events overtake you.

## Rude awakenings are painful

It helps if you have a roadmap with a clear intent to adopt state-of-art technologies. Too many companies bask in the glories of their past achievements. They often have a rude awakening as a tsunami of disruptions hits them; it is not an uncommon occurrence. Many companies presume to be agile or at least strive to achieve some level of agility level but frequently remain unaware, unprepared, or ill-equipped.

Such companies characteristically have little situational awareness, a weak drive to grasp the broader ecosystem's changes, and inadequate motivation to explore future scenarios. They relegate innovation to the periphery by creating a separate innovation arm within the company. Confining innovation to a corner is the best way to kill it, lose creativity, and forego the alternative of adapting to the emerging revolutions worldwide. Such companies fear emerging new technologies, new practices, and new ideas that could jeopardize their revenue stream. They are so busy doing the wrong thing that they don't have the time to do the right things.

## Situational awareness

So, what is situational awareness? Situational awareness is about intelligently understanding all the moving pieces in a fast-paced environment, its implications in the short-term and the long-term, and taking actions to mitigate the impacts.

Robert, an owner of a yoga school, noticed that a customer had ranked an experience with one of its coaches a low one-star on Yelp. The review piqued his curiosity, and he sought the details about the situation. He shared the customer feedback with the concerned coach to determine whether it was an odd failing or reflected an unnoticed pattern. Robert decided to understand the bigger picture based on the complaint and address the issue holistically.

Situational awareness has been widely used in aviation, healthcare, and the military for many years as a management precept. Miniaturization, increasingly aided by nanotechnology, has accelerated the adoption of situational awareness technologies in these sectors. The benefits of situational awareness are significant—an improvement in the quality of delivery, safe workplaces, organizational performance assurance, future-proofed product, and consumer acceptance as the most important of outcomes. By contrast, in the technology sector, we tend to fall into a routine until we are hit by a catastrophe, despite the availability of a wide variety of tools, practices, and technologies to confidently deal with the future.

## COVID-agility

Can we talk about COVID-agility and force majeure in the same breath? It sounds like an oxymoron —you would expect systems to be paralyzed by a disaster of this magnitude. Well, I am using a new word, aren't I? Let me first define this word. COVID-agility is about carefully and thoughtfully departing from a preconceived plan and adopting some agile precepts to meet the challenging demands of the pandemic, which brought the world to a standstill. COVID-agility could adapt fast enough to overcome a pandemic and not suffer the wreckage that it inflicted on work, life, and societies. It is not unthinkable that systems can be agile enough to cope with such a catastrophe in the digital age.

A few sectors, mostly technology, thrived during the crisis, which provides a glimmer of hope on how to cope. An elastic digital infrastructure affords enormous latitude to scale and soften the blow from external shocks. What is less certain is our ability to think creatively and adapt our work cultures, organizations, and societies to anticipate and respond at the speed of COVID-19 and its mutating strains. The worst-case scenario should draw on our collective wisdom and recreate sturdy systems for the future.

Amazon boomed during the pandemic as it quickly scaled to respond to the spike in demand for e-commerce, while the brick-and-mortar stores remained closed because their customers were restricted from in-person shopping or were less willing to do so. The rub was that Amazon's vendors' factories were not necessarily digitized enough to increase supply fast enough.

Rapid testing could have mitigated the risk of disease and kept many shops, businesses, and manufacturing plants open. However, traditional polymerase chain reaction (PCR) testing does not scale—the need to send swabs to centralized laboratories and treat them with chemical reagents, which are scarce during the crisis, is much too slow and vulnerable to supply chain disruptions for COVID agility.

## Speed accelerators

Speed matters in business. The world needs the immediacy and convenience akin to pregnancy tests. Point-of-care testing, especially testing that uses biosensors, is COVID-agile. It integrates with digital technologies that help to read the electrical signals from biomarkers or pathogens and send the data for analysis to centralized locations. These tests are convenient and cheap enough to repeat them frequently. Yet, the Centers for Disease Control was planning to expand PCR testing availability and only later turned its attention to funding point-of-care diagnostics, including nano-fluidics projects (tiny devices for testing).

## Workplaces of the future

Workplaces reshaped by the pandemic unfolded the future right in front of us faster than we could have imagined. Even as the world struggled to come to terms with the new way of life brought about by COVID, work-from-home became a part of the social fabric, with half the wages paid between May and October 2020 going to remote workers.

Networks adapted to the workforce's needs with collaboration technologies to keep communities productive. Some corporate leaders have recognized that work-from-home is a permanent trend that will alter the routines of a significant share of the workforce, blurring the work/family boundaries. Some innovations will meet the needs of home-based workers. Others such as holography and virtual reality, will likely make remote work as acceptable as on-premises face-to-face communication.

Communication and collaboration between home offices were soon overwhelmed by an overflow of traffic. The strain was relieved by SaaS products, which obviated the need to establish private VPN connections. Instead, employees used the cloud to access core services such as Microsoft Office suites (Office 365, G Suite) and collaboration software (Microsoft Teams, Slack). Commercial entities easily cope with spikes in traffic by taking recourse in cloud computing. At the last mile, their data centers are interconnected directly with cloud computing, or interconnection specialists such as Equinix provide conduits to route their traffic through private cloud networks. They do not have to suffer the congestion of the public Internet, which is a barrier to COVID agility.

## Breaks in the digital chain

By contrast, telecom service providers serve homes, and they have lagged in virtualizing their networks. Central offices, the aggregation point for traffic from homes, could very well house nodes for cloud computing, but they have been hamstrung by their hardware-based infrastructure, which does not scale for COVID agility.

Face-to-face communications are much valued, especially when human creativity is the main source of value creation. Situations such as product development and the crafting of messages for a market launch need direct human communication. Netflix CEO Reed Hastings recently said, "I don't see any positives. Not being able to get together in person, particularly internationally, is a pure negative." Goldman Sachs CEO David Solomon believes: "Our firm has always had a team-oriented apprenticeship culture, and we benefit from being and working together."

## Small and fleet-footed

Whatever the merits of each of these strategies, companies need more options to gain COVID agility. Management theorists have long recommended a cellular organizational structure with small teams led by their more entrepreneurial professionals. Many of the more talented workers leave large corporations when they find little opportunity to grow within their hierarchical organizations. Instead, they could flourish by becoming leaders of teams that are distributed across locations, mostly self-contained, able to meet each other locally and infrequently interact, face-to-face, with other company units.

The halting response that we have witnessed to the COVID-19 pandemic underscores the need to understand the complex and interdependent reality. COVID-agility will be possible only if we reimagine the workplace as a team of teams or a network connected by synergies. To sustain productivity, collaboration, and learning, the boundaries between being physically in the office and out of the office must blur altogether to convert futuristic ideas into standard practice. Technology is ready to help us achieve our goals, but not if we overlook organizational design.

## Oddballs prepare us for the future

It is a new awakening for all of us. My early career was in software development, and technical minutiae took so much of my time that I did not see the significance of systems thinking, the power of dynamically interlinked systems, and agile coaching back then. Centuries of grunt work has lulled our humanity and kept us from realizing the full power of our creativity.

We need a culture that revels in thinking outside-the-box, tolerates the oddballs among us, welcomes outliers, and is indulgent toward failures. Curiosity and experimentation should become a way of our lives. Agile coaches can contribute much by nurturing such cultures and encouraging attitudes that cherish innovation.

Change is a constant, and adaptive behaviors should be second nature among employees, management, and partners. Businesses, at the peak of their success, and established corporate houses are still wary of upstarts and new forms of automation because a big ship does not have a small flotilla's maneuverability. They still need to be prepared for market upheavals caused by groundbreaking technological change.

## Paying attention

There is a scene at the beginning of *The Bourne Identity* in which the film's protagonist is sitting in a restaurant, trying to figure out who he is and why he is being pursued by assassins. He doesn't understand why he has a bunch of passports and a gun stashed in a safe-deposit box. Bourne also realizes that he notices things that other people don't.

You don't have to be a ninja, such as Jason Bourne, to be situationally aware; you only need to be an avid learner, customer-obsessed, and data-driven to be as alert.

Technology has democratized knowledge. Some of the best content in the market is available for free at your fingertips. Use those to your advantage and understand the system that you operate in.

The customer is the source of innovation. Investors and customers are more aware, which prompts them to be more demanding of accountability. Failing companies, shorted by droves of traders, are quickly undermined and put their very existence at risk. Get closer to the customer. Look for a thousand ways to interact with them to know and serve them better.

And finally, you must be data-driven. Create the environment, tools, techniques, and a culture that acts on data.

## Who should read this book?

This book intends to raise situational awareness of the forces that are shaping our world and make your job as coach and leader more meaningful. A reading of this book will help you and your team imbue the right mindset and achieve great results.

This book is an effort to make industry leaders, coaches, and software professionals situationally aware and motivate them to more creatively tackle challenges in their journey. All leaders, coaches, and professionals should understand all the critical changes in business and society around us and the context that they are operating under. Situational awareness and creativity go hand in hand.

This book's intended audience is agile enthusiasts who want to understand how their profession has gained prominence. Professionals who seek answers to the following questions are likely to be interested:

- What underlies the urgency that propels all companies to be agile?
- How can we lead the situationally aware agile transformation?
- Why do investors who demand fast growth, and threats from competitors, require a rapid response to fast-changing realities?

# INTRODUCTION

Risk-hardened and shock-proof leaders and organizations will blaze the future trail. Exponential technologies and market upheavals, precipitous downturns, endemic risk and uncertainty, and black swan events have become overriding considerations in shaping business strategy, social organization, and workforce routines.

Companies and societies will absorb the shocks with pervasive elasticity and redundancy, virtual communications and collaboration across their ecologies, immersion in data, and COVID- agility. Strategic frameworks would have to advance to discount not only both the short and medium prospects, but future risks. Analytics and scenario planning will arm companies and societies to foresee their challenges and not be caught off-guard.

Adversity is the mother of resilience and the innovation to emerge from it. Those who survive also get a head start in taking advantage of an economic upturn and emerging opportunities. Agile companies calibrate and reinvent their business models to tread unchartered waters in anticipation of unexpected opportunities. Those who have turned adverse situations to their advantage uncommonly reap disproportionate rewards.

Technology is fragile. A significant outage leaves millions of users stranded. Today's information technology infrastructure embodies sophisticated methods to continue operations despite the higher risk of breakdowns. Interconnected systems are prone to catastrophic cascading disasters. Virtualized resources such as storage and servers have their twins across geographies and can instantaneously switch traffic as machines break down. The practice has evolved with the IoT, which detects signals about machines' health and predicts disaster scenarios from the historical data to complete maintenance even before a machine breaks down. Similarly, our organizations and societies need the ability to read weak (and strong) signals to adapt, recreate, and rebuild as situations change.

Historically, companies are reactive; they resign themselves to periodic recessions and make changes only after they suffer setbacks in downturns. A study of the response to recessions concluded that a small minority of companies who anticipated and pre-emptively took action to mitigate the impact of recessions not only grew faster during and after the recession, but they realized higher rates of return. Recessions are also an opportunity to benefit from emerging trends that lead to the expansion of new markets. Conversely, the firms who do not change experience setbacks and long-term damage because they do not build customer equity, and their markets grow slowly or come to a screeching halt sooner or later.

Business is all about risk management. Risk and uncertainty, of many different types, is endemic in today's world. The business environment is refashioned or redefined by significant risk events. Companies that cope with market upheavals with creative solutions are often the leaders in the marketplace. They get a head start over incumbents.

An unexpected oil price hike in the 1970s rocked the automobile industry. Those who gained redesigned their cars to radically improve their thermodynamics. There was no way that companies could have survived with the old designs. Japanese vehicles quickly brought reliable, utilitarian vehicles for customers looking for good value for their money, and thrived. Old-style cars from Detroit lost market shares.

In the current environment, electric cars are rapidly replacing the old mechanical vehicles. Incumbents such as GM and German manufacturers such as BMW have no choice but to follow in the footsteps of Tesla.

In each of these cases, alert observers could see the writing on the wall but did not sink into the corporate world's zeitgeist due to inertia, the fear of the unknown, and sunk costs. The oil price hike was inevitable as an environment of low oil prices depressed investments in exploration. Declining battery prices, shorter time to recharge, and increasing range make electric cars competitive with those powered by fossil fuels.

Businesses and societies need to future-proof their strategies to sustain growth over the long run and absorb external shocks. Short-term business planning horizons overlook the enormous costs of long-term damage to reputation and the risk of bankruptcy. Long supply chains meant to keep product prices low exposed their vulnerability during the COVID-19 crisis when critical supply items such as personal protective equipment dried up when desperately needed.

Quick adjustments to external shocks are possible today in an environment of digital platforms, processes, and ecologies. Multiple platforms can complement their distributed capabilities to serve newly discovered needs. Companies and societies need access to databases to learn about a vastly more extensive range of human skills, technologies, knowledge, and resources than within their organizations and platforms. They also need new management and negotiation skills to rebuild teams to serve purposes that change with external shocks, technological change, and market shifts.

Another exciting technology that *Financial Times* suggests could be larger than the Internet, while others dismiss it as an extravagant hype, is additive manufacturing, also known as 3D printing. 3D printing came to the rescue of some hospitals because it could rapidly scale to meet the local needs for personal protective equipment. Stay-at-home Government policies did not hinder production of

3D equipment—workers in homes could manufacture personal protection equipment.

3D printing comes in handy in an emergency such as COVID, when restocking inventories is no longer predictable. Supplies of some products could unexpectedly run short when an unanticipated wave of infections hits their manufacturing clusters. Because 3D printing can quickly reset machines to manufacture a different product, it can supplement inventories from traditional sources to fully meet demand.

3D printing also makes work-from-home viable for manufacturing with distributed and collaborative manufacturing with cloud computing. A distributed team of engineers can design a product on a single interface using the cloud. A 3D printing farm, where a single factory supervises a collection of machines, can manufacture a diversity of products with multiple designs.

Individual 3D manufacturing facilities cannot manufacture the entire range of components in the assembly of products. Today, databases exist to discover the suppliers who offer parts with the attributes to meet demand at the lowest cost.

Even with the usual business flow, 3D printing adapts with greater agility to product and technological innovation. These machines reprogram to switch to new products without incurring the costs of retiring old machines.

In a world of social distancing and restricted air travel, remote assistance, augmented reality, and

3D software affords opportunities for global work-forces to collaborate without physical proximity. Nestle's Swiss workers could complete maintenance and build new plants by remotely assisting their peers overseas.

Several technologies designed to respond to crises with COVID-agility have not been brought into broader use because mental models are steeped in older ways of working. Telehealth is a classic example of a technology that can elastically increase capacity. It remained dormant for a long time until the turmoil of pandemic suddenly filled up space in hospitals, where capacity expansion is expensive. As a result, hospitals had to postpone urgent care for other diseases such as cancer. Telehealth remained at the periphery with only 1 percent of the market share before COVID. It then zoomed to 60 percent at the coronavirus's peak before stabilizing at around 20 percent in July 2020. In the past, doctors found telehealth underwhelming without the opportunity to see patients in person and the ability to examine and test for vital signs on-premise.

Beyond video conferencing for an initial examination, telehealth has expanded its remote examination and monitoring ability and testing. MedWand, among several others, has invented new tools for several virtual examinations and uses them at a chain of primary care centers, MedLion.

New models have emerged in which acute care at home, by companies such as Medically Home, in conjunction with remote telehealth, is now recognized by regulatory policy as a viable option for critical care. Pandemics and epidemics are recurring as diseases such as Ebola and SARS, or MERS, which were previously localized in some regions, quickly spread worldwide with ever-increasing air travel volumes. Telehealth can rapidly respond to spikes in demand for healthcare in such situations.

To prepare your organization for the future shaped by technology, you must start thinking now about an array of levers that might be in your operating domain that you can press to cope with challenges a few short months from now.

Scenario planning is a structured method to foresee how this future terrain could turn out for you. The prospect of a nuclear attack and the potential devastation of communications networks sparked the idea of an Internet. The US military concluded that centralized networks of the day would crumble in a nuclear attack. Scenario planning for the future should consider the vulnerabilities in the interdependent digital systems. They should evaluate the impact that disasters can have on our workplaces' communications, collaboration, and remote control; each of them should be tested for resilience under alternative scenarios grounded in understanding future challenges.

## How is this book organized?

"Why doesn't my washing machine start?"

"Why won't my computer work?"

Those are among the frequently asked questions

(FAQ) contained in owner's manuals. People don't want to wade through pages of directions after buying a product, especially if the directions are hard to understand or follow. This book does not have an FAQ section, so you might want to read the book from cover to cover. You may miss the thread in the book if you skip or skim the preface, which discusses the critical concepts.

The first chapter, "The changing paradigm of the new economy," will give an overview of all the transformations that compel industry, society, and business to respond. Those changes effectively shrink the world by connecting us in new ways, re-imagining the workplace environment, revolutionizing manufacturing, reinventing business, changing customer behavior, advancing healthcare, and experiencing new realities. For the first time in history, more than half of the world's population is living in cities. A new digital generation has emerged with its distinct attitudes and preferences, driving the rewriting of business rules. The exponential progress in technology has brought us close to an abundant future, which was unthinkable before.

The second chapter talks about how the industrial world is transforming into a digital world. The digital transformation is at the center of four prevailing technology foundations: cloud, social, mobile, and big data. These foundational technologies and new accelerators such as AI, IoT, blockchain, nanotechnology, and 3D printing could create many new future scenarios. You will be introduced to some of those future scenarios that have already begun to affect business and society in more than one way.

The third chapter highlights the second coming of customization and mass personalization. New platform technologies give a highly personalized digital experience for specific types of customers. As some people would say, platforms are eating the world—a new paradigm in which value is created and distributed among participants outside of the traditional enterprise. Platforms attract both consumers and suppliers, and the information and interactions between the participants become a source of value creation. As the number of participants increases, so does the value of platforms, a phenomenon known as the "network effect."

The fourth chapter goes into the details of Platform 2.0 and the network effect of intersecting technologies. Multi-technology platforms and network technologies are increasingly affecting individual businesses and have broader impacts on industries, economies, societies, and communities.

The last chapter dives deeper into the "how" part of the transformation. It talks about the mental models to clarify transformation goals and using digital ways of working and digital interactions that are revolutionizing the way we do business. Shared mental models are critical for collaboration, focus, and keeping pace with a fast-changing world. Successful organizations have adopted new mental models to thrive in the new world. They have shifted their attitude, orientation, and priorities to move quickly in a world where the big does not eat the small, but the fast eats the slow.

# CHAPTER 1

## The changing paradigm of the new economy

Against the backdrop of successive waves of innovation that ensued after the collapse of the Internet boom, all businesses need a perspective on how they will adapt to emerging futures if they do not want to perish. Understanding the technical elements is essential, but it is crucial to be aware of the organizational and social impact. The remaking of our world affects our lifestyles, workplaces, and interactions. We need new mental models to adapt to this world. Examples of some of the mental models are gaining speed, interacting digitally, using a data-driven approach, being customer-obsessed, becoming future-ready, and building the future enterprise. Later we will talk about some of the heuristics companies are using to succeed with digital transformation.

Ironically, the IT sector neither absorbs new mental models nor unlearns old habits fast enough. Companies that seek to gain a stronger position in the marketplace must develop situational awareness and build a few mental models to help them grapple with transformation. Additionally, they need to figure out the right business model, the right customers and partners, and the new abnormal strategy.

Let's look at some of the remarkable changes that have already happened in the last two decades.

## Globally local

The world has become less distant since the 1990s, and digital transformation amplifies the trend as interactive communication and collaboration among people worldwide become as routine as logging on to a computer every day. People are more aware of the tastes, preferences, and lifestyles of citizens in other countries. Starbucks in China, Zara clothes and Nike sneakers, Korean cars, Chinese mobile phones and furniture, Wal-Mart supermarkets worldwide, French retail chain Fnac in Rio—this is globalization entrenched in our daily lives.

Back in 1990, the worldwide volume of foreign travel was about 400 million trips. That included business travelers, tourists, and students studying abroad. Today, the number has almost tripled, with 1.1 billion journeys. Globalization and interconnectedness bring the benefit of sourcing the best talent, the best ideas, and the best inputs from anywhere in the world. It enables countries to specialize in what they do best. Overall, competition drives a faster pace of change.

The reach of millions of small businesses extends to the rest of the world as they communicate, collaborate, and trade on platforms such as Facebook, and Alibaba of China. They can no longer view their universe as limited to their nation-states, but it extends to the world in which they have customers.

## Exponential change

The pioneer of the digital piano, Ray Kurzweil, posited the "The Law of Accelerating Returns"—driven by exponential, rather than linear, progress in technology. He asserts that the 21st century is a singularity moment—it will be a time of liftoff with 20,000 years of evolution compressed in a single century. In the next few decades, machine intelligence will surpass human intelligence. The fusion of biological and non-biological intelligence, nanotechnology, software-augmented humans, and ultra-high intelligence, which processes information at the speed of light, will turbocharge progress. The predicate of the idea of exponential technological change is that the massive volumes of data from three universes—the human genome project, nanotechnology, and robotic intelligence—will swell to planetary dimensions as they interact with each other. Nanotechnology, for example, needs artificial intelligence (AI) to piece together the nanoparticles to form new materials. The more AI progresses, the greater will be the advances in developing new materials.

Biology has inspired algorithms such as deep-learning neural networks that take cues from the brain's neural interconnections and synapses between them to parse data and find patterns and make predictions. Genetic algorithms have taken cues from evolutionary biology to string together components, such as in FPGA chips, that fit best in a more complex system to achieve the desired outcomes.

Genetic algorithms, in turn, are used to diagnose complex diseases such as cancer. Mammograms, CT scans, and X-rays detect breast cancer. Images captured from multiple angles cumulatively add up to enormous volumes of hard data for humans to decipher. Genetic algorithms help to find the fits in the individual pieces of data to come to a precise understanding of the mutations in malignant tumors well before they threaten life. They help to separate healthy cells from those that are pathogenic.

## A hare wins, and the tortoise loses

In business, the new mantra is "The fast eat the slow." Speedy responses win in an environment of fickle customers who feast on creative customization that pops up on their Facebook wall after a browser search. Zara's, the world's largest fashion retailer, has super-fast inventory turnarounds that the New York Times characterized as "mind-spinningly supersonic." Zara's is quick to respond to its customers' preferences; it ships products to stores twice a week. The cycle time for Zara's in-house design team is three weeks from the design kickoff to the start of manufacturing on the shop floor.

Unlike most retailers, Zara stocks only a part of its inventory, six months in advance, for all its season demand. Most retailers lock in 100 percent of an upcoming season's stock to ensure a predictable supply and protection against price spikes closer to the start of a season. Zara reserves only 15 to 25 percent of inventory six months in advance, according to tradegecko.com. It leaves enough room to adapt to unanticipated changes in demand during the season. Typically, its inventory level rises to 50 or 60 percent of the expected sale by the start of the season. The remaining 40 to 50 percent of sales swoop on unanticipated opportunities during the season. Zara manufactures 50 percent of its supply in Spain, Portugal, Turkey, and Morocco, instead of China, to shorten the delivery time.

Despite its long reign as a market leader, Black-Berry's demise illustrates the harmful effect of slow responses. After Apple launched its first iPhone in 2007, the CEO of Research in Motion (which owned BlackBerry) famously commented: "Why would anyone want to watch a video on the phone?" His guileless reaction to Apple's emergence betrayed just how blind he was to the emerging future. The failure to understand a significant market trend is often the reason for the undoing of market-dominating companies.

Economies of scale were the cornerstone of the industrial economy. Corporations saw that as the *sine qua non* of competitive advantage. They could afford slow responses due to their entrenched cost advantage and overlooked distribution channels, suppliers, and other competitive strengths.

The current business landscape has few of the dominant players that existed in 2000. Overall, 52 percent of the companies once on the Fortune 500 companies list have perished, unable to adapt because they were not agile enough. Accelerating technological changes shorten the lifespan of products, business models, and companies. According to Innosight, 75 percent of the companies listed on the S&P 500 will disappear from the index by 2027.

## The customer: reading the pulse

*Rapid scaling is often necessary for high-technology startups because low entry barriers allow competitors to grab market share and eventually overtake first movers. However, if startups cannot scale, entrepreneurs should fail fast. For entrepreneurs with high opportunity costs, pivoting to a new idea can be more efficient than persistence in a lost cause.* (Arora and Nandkumar, 2011)

We have moved on from realizing business value to customer value with a shift from the product to the customer. Value creation happens when customers use products, not when a business delivers a product. And value creation does not end there. It extends into LTV (lifetime value of the customer)— serving customers in all aspects and retaining them for a lifetime.

Most companies claim they know their customers, but they rarely make them their cynosure. Unlike Amazon, customer service is not a driving passion for organizations. The shifts in technology and customer tastes warrant a granular understanding of customer behavior to maximize customer value. Companies should make it a habit to reference customers in their decision-making. They should create war rooms to find ways to gather critical customer data and announce key breakthroughs in customer acquisition and retention to encourage attention to customers' needs.

Nordstrom is one company that has embraced a Scrum-team approach, providing undivided attention to serving customers and enhancing products to consistently win customers over. A classic case was how it set up a temporary camp in its flagship store, and a team launched a series of weeklong experiments to perfect a new app for its sunglasses. The app guides customers through the selection process by matching sunglasses styles with a customer's facial characteristics and preferences.

Customers were presented with an early virtual version of the app and asked about the features they found helpful, unnecessary, or distracting. Based on that feedback, the team's coders built a live version of the app for customers to test, making real-time adjustments as they received more input. After a week of tweaking, they released it on tablets to the store's sales associates, who use it alongside customers to help them choose sunglasses.

PayPal had not planned to be a disruptor in online payment service. In her book, *Founders at Work*, Jessica Livingston spoke to PayPal founder Max Levchin, who revealed that PayPal set out a cryptography company. Later, it experimented with transferring money using PDAs. After years of experimentation, PayPal settled on online payment as its sweet spot for millions of people.

A study by Harvard professors concluded: "We find that A/B testing is associated with a 5-15% increase in website visits and is positively correlated with increased product introductions, code changes, and other performance metrics."

## Zero marginal cost–the age of abundance

In his book *Abundance*, Peter Diamandis talks about rapid *demonetization*—the cost of living approaching near zero. That means that we can meet our basic needs at negligible expense. Accelerated diffusion of technologies in housing, transportation, food, health care, entertainment, clothing, and education reduces costs to a rounding error.

Until recently, phone calls were a substantial part of your monthly bills, especially international communication. WhatsApp, Skype, Facebook Messenger, and Google Hangout virtually allow you to make free phone calls anywhere.

Demonetization has already happened in several sectors of the economy. Craigslist demonetized classified ads; iTunes's Spotify did that for the music industry; Airbnb for hotels; Schwab, Wealthfront, Betterment, and Robinhood for investments; and Amazon for bookstores. Mass open online colleges demonetized education. Housing (office space) could be demonetized by a distributed workforce using virtual reality. There are several attempts such as that of Winsun in China, which tried to 3D print an entire apartment building.

## Costless education

Online learning is not the future anymore, especially after the pandemic. The asynchronous mode and anytime, anywhere learning is helping students reach new heights. Students are enrolling in free massive open online courses (MOOC). The world of online education is getting bigger and better, with platforms such as Coursera, Udacity, and Khan Academy offering hundreds of free, high-quality courses. Many universities are also beginning to offer open courses online (see Yale and MIT). Stanford professors founded Coursera and Udacity.

As tuition rates continue to skyrocket and quality content is available for free, the new trend in education empowers those who cannot afford soaring education costs. Quality online education is becoming a viable alternative to a traditional degree, forcing institutions to re-imagine themselves. MOOCs' appeal for both professors and students is so powerful that it just might change higher education for good. MOOCs are designed to be scalable to large online masses with free participation and with no formal requirements, and provide millions of people with the opportunity to learn through hundreds of public and private universities or organizations worldwide.

## Crowdsourcing–Zen-like

*It takes a village to raise a child.—African proverb*

Crowdsourcing is the means to source information, access gig workers, or obtain funding from a village (or a bunch of people) in a Zen-like fashion with distributed control. Crowd-like approaches to creativity and idea generation, such as jams, hackathons, idea marketplaces, and personal entrepreneurial projects, may increase the scope for innovation and flexibility inside companies. They are qualitatively different and fall short of the full capability of external crowds.

Crowdsourcing as a problem-solving tool has existed, in one form or another, for centuries. Communities of innovators have helped kick-start aviation and personal computing. Their zeal solved some of the most complex scientific problems in history, including the effort to map longitude and latitude at sea.

Britain's Parliament established the Longitude Prize in 1714 after a host of crème de la crème scientists, including Giovanni Domenico Cassini, Christiaan Huygens, Edmond Halley, and Isaac Newton, tried in vain to find an answer. The winning solution, one of more than 100 submissions, came from a humble carpenter and clockmaker from the English countryside, John Harrison, who eventually won an award of about £15,000. He invented a highly accurate chronometer (watch) that enabled the exact triangulation of location.

Technology has changed the nature of crowdsourcing today. It creates a community of eager beavers. An innate desire to learn and shine among the community of peers energizes crowds.

In LEGO's Ideas platform, users submit innovative ideas for new LEGO sets. Suppose the idea receives a lot of votes from the community. In that case, the selected candidate gets an opportunity to collaborate with the LEGO team to make his or her idea a reality and earn royalties. More than idea generation, this approach validates customers' needs, one of the fundamentals of agility.

My Starbucks Idea is a platform for crowdsourcing customer and barista suggestions, in which almond milk was one of the top requests a few years ago. Starbucks finally introduced its own proprietary Starbucks almond milk, yielding to customer demand.

PepsiCo solicited consumer opinion on new potato chip flavors for the company's Lay's brand. It has received millions of submissions—Cheesy Garlic Bread was the winner in 2013. An 8 percent increase in sales followed this crowdsourcing innovation campaign.

Amazon allows anyone to submit concept videos and scripts. Amazon Preview is an invite-only community that provides feedback on test-footage, storyboards, and concepts. Pilot Season is another group on Amazon that enables users to watch television show pilots for free while voting to commission some for a full season.

## Kickstart the social fund

Crowdfunding is socialized funding that bypasses financial intermediaries to raise money directly from savers. Digital platforms, such as Kickstarter or Indiegogo, connect social entrepreneurs with small savers who want to donate for a future reward. Crowdfunder and WeFunder, among others, are conduits for equity crowdfunding.

Some social groups, previously starved of capital, can now raise it over crowdfunding platforms. It is possible to raise funds for purposes other than capital investments; iFundWomen funds women-led startups and small businesses. A biologist at the University of Sussex raised almost £8,000 to screen for pesticides in random plant samples from garden centers. Kal Penn, the actor best known for his roles in the medical TV show *House* and the Harold and Kumar film series, raised more than $800,000 for Syrian refugees.

Some of the startups who raised money from crowdfunding campaigns went on to blaze new trails:

- Oculus pioneered the wearable virtual reality space, raised money on Kickstarter, and was later acquired by Facebook for $2 billion in 2014.
- SkyBell raised $600,000 in a 30-day campaign on Indiegogo for its smart video doorbell, which sends live video of a homeowner's front door to their smartphone.

- Pebble was one of the pioneers of smartwatches and raised more than $10 million from nearly 69,000 backers on Kickstarter.

## Disintermediation

The dot-com boom in the 1990s ushered in an era of disintermediation epitomized by the travel industry. Technology-mediated direct booking with airlines and hotels replaced travel agents, because customers preferred competitive pricing, transparency, and a broader choice.

In recent years, disintermediation has extended to banking and financial services. New digital entrantssuch as Nutmeg, TransferWise, PayPal, and Venmo take on core bank functions such as lending, investing, payments, money transfer, and providing free online financial advice. Square and Braintree allow small businesses to accept payments.

Digital giants such as Google, Apple, and Alibaba are offering their payment services Google Wallet, Apple Pay, and AliPay. They allow you to transfer funds to beneficiaries without a bank account.

The transaction costs of services supplied by digital companies are near zero. Simple and BankMobile provide banking with no fees. Robo-advisors Acorns, Betterment, Wealthfront, and Robinhood do not charge commissions for stock trades, portfolio management tools, and automated investing.

Small businesses have an alternative to the excruciating credit evaluation processes used by banks. LendingClub, eToro (not in the US), CAN Capital, Kabbage, and Fundera (matching people with lenders) use analytics for credit scoring without even so much as a customer's visit to a bank branch.

## B2C to C2B to C2C

Business models have undergone a paradigm shift; instead of pushing products to consumers, and instead of marketing existing inventory stocks to manufacturing, they are demand-driven.

Today, business models have a short shelf life. The game's basic rules for creating and capturing economic value lasted for prolonged periods; competitors tweaked them to remain in the marketplace. Increasingly, new business models catch the incumbents by surprise. Some examples are as follows:

- Bitcoin bypasses traditional banks and clearinghouses with blockchain technology.
- Coursera and edX, among others, threaten business schools with MOOCs.
- Tencent gained an edge with a higher-margin microtransaction business combined with digital products and services, such as computer games.
- Uber sidesteps the medallion system that protects taxicab franchises in cities around the world.

Users of digital services do not just passively consume, but are also active contributors and co-creators. A member of Vimeo can upload videos and purchase premium versions of content created by others. Similarly, a user of Facebook could also advertise there. A household can both consume electricity generated by its solar panel and sell it to the grid.

A fundamental change from acquiring and hoarding knowledge to spreading and sharing it is affecting different industries. For example, Skillshare provides a platform in which professionals share their knowledge and earn a second income while acquiring knowledge from their work with customers. Scientific expertise in life sciences is about developing new knowledge from laboratory investigations and mining available databases to repurpose old drugs for new uses.

The subscription economy explosion is spreading from flowers to cloud computing to data storage to beauty care products. At Schiphol airport, Philips offers lighting-as-a-service; it owns the bulbs, and the airport pays for the service. The lines between manufacturing and services are blurring. Rolls-Royce no longer sells jet engines; it sells the hours each of its engines uses to power an airplane while it is in flight.

Time-tested, predictable systems have given way to complex adaptive systems. Traditional marketing research and campaigns are still widely used, but they capture information in a single period or specific contexts. By contrast, social media interaction can use various platforms to interact with customers from multiple segments, in different periods, and moods created by events. They provide an opportunity to adapt by learning from feedback received from quantitative data and the buzz.

## Mass personalization—commonly unique

AI and machine learning are enabling mass personalization across many industries. Amazon tailors its offers based on a user's past purchases, interests, and searches. For example, when you log in to Amazon, it shows "Get yourself a little something" or books "Based on your readings" or "Contemporary picks for you." Similarly, Netflix suggests movies based on your interest, genre, artists, and more.

Social media interaction complements customized marketing. It is a quick way to gauge market trends and to reconfigure products and services to adapt to fleeting movements in the marketplace. TikTok, for example, collects engagement and customer data to refine and rinse its algorithms. The feedback loop, referred to as the "virtuous cycle of AI," continuously feeds new information to make better recommendations even when content consumers do not necessarily explicitly articulate their preferences.

Companies such as Pega and ClickFox track customers at each of their touchpoints to trace their customer journey and influence them with messages, rewards, and content. They make product recommendations as the customer comes close to the end of the purchase journey.

Participation of customers in product development is another way to personalize products. Pepperidge Farm customers now design Goldfish crackers. Trek provides customers with a configurator for prospective customers to pick their choice of components and paint. And Brooks Brothers allows men to create their own suits.

L'Oréal's Makeup Genius app takes these capabilities to a whole new level by virtualizing customers' appearances that go with the makeup of their choice. As the app tracks a customer's responses to products, it learns about the psychology of similar customers' preferences. Customers complete the path from consideration to purchase because an enjoyable experience engages customers. With 14 million users already, the app has become a critical asset both as a branded channel for engaging with customers and as a firehose of incoming information on how customers engage.

## The hyperlinked generation

Two widely used terms—digital natives and digital immigrants—distinguish two modes of thinking in the digital era. Digital natives, a term coined by US author Marc Prensky, characterizes people who grew up during the digital age, and digital immigrants were born before the advent of digital technology.

Technological culture shapes the attitudes and preferences of each of them. The digital natives' world is egalitarian and horizontal, not hierarchical; they reject centralized and control-based corporate governance. Many of their traits are inherently agile; they function best when networked, and they thrive on instant gratification and frequent rewards. They love sharing things and ideas and across boundaries. Many of them not only question traditional institutions and rules, but rewrite those rules.

As with the digital natives, digital immigrants are goal-oriented rather than value-oriented. Digital immigrants learn to adapt to their environment, but retain their foot in the past. They still like to print an e-mail and do math without much help from a calculator. In an Agile space, they prefer to physically collaborate with people instead of using digital collaboration tools such as Trello, Zoom, Jira, and Asana.

Text messaging (SMS), for example, was developed in the 1980s as an easy way for service engineers to quickly communicate about outages and replacement parts. Back then, no one could foresee that young people would chat using an instant messenger service, or use Twitter instead of talking on the phone. These two world views, in combination, produced, for better or worse, a new form of communication and a multibillion-dollar industry. If we allow an opening for an ongoing dialogue between these two generations, we can all achieve things that we wouldn't otherwise be able to do.

## A tale of a million cities

As recently as 2000, 95 percent of the Fortune Global 500 companies had their headquarters in developed economies. By 2025, when China will be home to more large companies than either the United States or Europe, we expect nearly half of the world's large companies—defined as those with revenue of $1 billion or more—to be headquartered in emerging markets.

The global urban population has been rising by an average of 65 million people annually during the past three decades, the equivalent of adding seven Chicagos a year. Nearly half of global GDP growth between 2010 and 2025 will come from 440 cities in emerging markets—95 percent of them small- and medium-sized cities that many Western executives may not even have heard of and couldn't point to on a map. Yes, Mumbai, Dubai, and Shanghai are now familiar names.

More than half of the world's population currently resides in cities, and the number is likely to swell to 66 percent by 2050, according to the United Nations.

## The new way of working
Two forces are influencing the new way of working: the spread of automation and the human cloud. Gig workers constitute the human cloud; online workplaces such as oDesk, Hired, or Upwork interconnect millions of them, all rated by their previous employers. HourlyNerd rents out former consultants and top business-school graduates to help with strategic planning, financial analysis, and other high-level tasks; customers range from small- and

medium-sized businesses to top companies such as Microsoft.

Students today will do jobs that don't currently exist; they have not yet been conceptualized. One California-based school, High Tech High, is preparing students for the uncertain future. The co-founder of the school, Larry Rosenstock, wants kids to do the work that's important to them, making them prepare for the future instead of following an antiquated scholastic routine.

High Tech High is a model of how formal education can embrace inquiry-based, truly student-driven, project-based learning. The school promotes creativity, pragmatism, and collaborative work. Larry Rosenstock wants to achieve a goal versus a mad rush for high test scores.

# CHAPTER 2

## Bienvenue–the future has arrived

The world is advancing from an industrial economy to a digital economy, reshaping the landscape in which we live and work. We have outlined a framework below to encapsulate the salient features that we need to grasp to master the new reality. In the table below, you can see how the industrial economy is changing into a digital economy for each of the pointers.

| Pointers | Industrial Economy | Digital Economy |
|---|---|---|
| Economic Development | Steady, linear, predictable | Volatile, disruptive |
| Market Changes | Slow and linear | Fast and unpredictable |
| Lifecycle of Products/ Technology | Long | Short |
| Key Economy Drivers | Large industrial firms | Innovative, adaptive firms |
| Competition | The big eats the small | The fast eats the slow |
| Business Approach | Vision, goals, action plans | Opportunistic, dynamic |
| Source of Competitive Advantage | Cheap labor, capital, scale | Speed, partnership |
| Organizational Structures | Hierarchical, bureaucratic | Flat or networked structure |
| Leadership | Command-and-control | Self-organized teams |
| Skills | Mono-skilled, manual labor | Multi-skilled, intelligence |

The convergence of four technologies—social, mobile, analytics and cloud—was driving business innovation and transforming e-business to digital business. Each of these forces on their own is a powerful agent for change, but in combination, they're more powerful. The intersection of these forces, also called digital transformation, has allowed some companies to go unhinged to solve real-world problems, because they don't feel shackled by current industry thinking.

## Social–sharing the sharing

Social means more than conversations on social media. The social aspects of a business are collaboration, interactions, co-creation, and socio-technical practices. People are undoubtedly the invaluable assets of any organization, and social technologies help unlock the knowledge in individuals' minds and disseminate that knowledge to drive business outcomes.

COVID-19 has dissolved the old conceptions of collaboration and interaction. Remote collaboration with global partners or those in geographically separated locations has been an accepted form of work for a couple of decades. Now the question is whether pervasive work-from-home is as normal as on-premises face-to-face communication.

Some forms of decision-making thrive when people can continuously interact and socialize within an office. There are other activities such as content writing, graphic design, and engineering that need intermittent collaboration. Functions such as product management, by contrast, create much of their value from frequent interaction.

Remote collaboration on the scale needed in the post-COVID environment requires a new operating model. Time windows for interaction for people across geographies are narrow, and synchronous communication is harder to accommodate as demands for organizing frequent meetings increase.

**The madness of crowds goes viral**

In our age, breaking events shape perceptions in split seconds, and masses of people react on social media before businesses have a chance to repair any damage that might have occurred or swim with the tide to benefit from it. Individuals and small groups of people sway opinion with panache as they touch nerves with provocative language.

In 2017, United Airlines inadvertently provoked outrage after forcibly removing a passenger from a seat to make room for a crew member. The video of the coerced removal went viral on social media the world over. United Airlines' stock fell as much as 4 percent the next day.

Earlier in 2009, musician Dave Carroll's expensive Taylor guitar was damaged by United Airlines' baggage handlers. Carroll, denied reimbursement by United, took to YouTube to spread the word with his video, "United Breaks Guitars," which was watched more than 11 million times by December 2011. *The Times Online* in the UK estimated that the negative publicity cost United more than $180 million in lost market cap.

McDonald's expected to earn accolades with a new version of its famous mascot with the hashtag #RonaldMcDonald, but the plan backfired when many of Twitter's responses bashed the clown's makeover and the restaurant chain's food. In an age when chef celebrities influence cooking, McDonald is an awkward mascot. Those who hate mass-produced food pounced and flooded social media with negative commentary about it. More than ever before, businesses have to be aware of digital culture and its influencers.

## Mobile—hello, I am everywhere

Retail shopping today is increasingly influenced by information distributed on mobile devices. People explore their options in spare moments when they are waiting at airports, waiting for doctors' appointments, or while traveling in a car or on public transportation. Facebook advertisements quickly show product information based on user searches. Depending on the product's nature, they can quickly find content on websites that help them make decisions. If they are planning to design their backyard landscape, they can use mobile applications to visualize and make up their minds.

InMobi, a global mobile advertising and discovery platform, found in a study that 80 percent of Asian mobile Internet users take advantage of mobile shopping. With the continued development and use of mobile devices, your company needs to adapt with the times and become mobile-friendly.

Mobile technologies are continuing to evolve, reshaping the technology landscape. Today's smartphones are immensely powerful devices—they are rapidly shrinking the percentage of unconnected adults globally (according to the research carried out by network experts Ericsson). The growth in smart devices is bringing about an era of ubiquitous connectivity. Users are now able to access information anywhere, anytime, with ease.

Gartner, Inc. forecasts that 8.4 billion connected things worldwide in 2017 will soon reach more than 20 billion, as people move beyond smartphones and tablets to embrace a wide array of mobile devices, including smart watches, medical devices, smart cars, and connected appliances.

## Cloud—convenience on demand

Cloud computing is like a grid, in which a broad set of services and data resides, and web browsers or applications present interfaces to control them. Today, cloud technology has become the new foundation of the IT ecosystem. Cloud computing lends businesses newfound agility, breaking down the barriers of geography and cutting the costs associated with physical server maintenance. With limitless scalability, the cloud powers the transformative combination of social, mobile, and analytic technologies.

## Big data, big promise

Big data and analytics are the engines of supply chains; they feed closed-loop marketing and optimize existing customer relationship management processes. They generate insights to inform smart boardroom decision-making in real-time. New, upcoming organizations are data-driven. They are relying more on data than on years of experience and the gut feeling of superiors. Companies that foster a culture of data-driven decisions, such as Amazon, will lead the revolutions in the years to come.

The use of anonymized big data sets has the potential to drive social change. For example, during the swine flu epidemic of 2009, Telefonica's digital research team used mobile phone data to track people's movements. The team found that the Mexican government's timely restrictions on people's movement around the country contained the flu spread.

But the best is yet to come. While the trend started a while ago, the new accelerators such as blockchain, AI, and IoT, along with future scenarios that emanate from the combination of all those forces, are performing complex cognitive tasks to solve real-world problems in ways that were previously unknown. All our senses—vision, sound, smell, taste, and touch—are converted to digital equivalents through sensors and data by the organizations.

## Blockchain—future of fintech?

Blockchain is a distributed ledger—a technology with an enormous innovation potential in financial services and other sectors such as identity management. A blockchain keeps permanent records of transactions interconnected and spread across individual blocks.

A public blockchain allows everyone to be present on the platform to read or write to the platform after being validated as trusted peers. A private blockchain allows only a subset of owners or an owner to have the right to make any changes to the platform to ensure the stored information's confidentiality. This concept has drawn considerable interest from financial industry members such as Goldman Sachs, Barclays, Citibank, and more.

People know blockchain by its most popular product—Bitcoin, the cryptocurrency built on open-source software. The foundation of Bitcoin is a decentralized ledger with built-in peer-to-peer oversight.

Trust is a much-sought-after attribute in the financial services industry, and distributed chains extend oversight into the far corners of their value chain. Blockchains are finding favor in the insurance industry to track and trace where, when, and how damage and loss occur.

Blockchain technology has additional identity management applications in passports, birth certificates, wedding certificates, IDs, and online account logins. A British company, Provenance, piloted blockchain to pioneer a new traceability method in tuna fishing to stop illegal fishing. It used mobile, blockchain, and smart tagging to track fish caught by fishermen from origin to the point of sale (POS).

## Artificial intelligence— incredibly accurate

Humans will be augmented by machines, contrary to the perception that machines will replace humans. Ultimately, humans and machines will collaborate to solve society's most significant challenges such as beating disease, ignorance, and poverty. As we automate everything, AI will combine human traits such as creativity, empathy, emotion, physicality, and insight.

A company called Touchpoint is developing a form of AI that it describes as "the world's angriest robot," designed to learn why customers become upset. Known as Radiant, the AI is reminiscent of Prime Radiant, a fictional cube from Isaac Asimov's *Foundation* series, capable of predicting human behavior.

## Cognitive Robotics

Cognitive robotics provides robots with perception, attention, anticipation, planning, memory, learning, and reasoning with AI. It can mimic human behavior that helps in service industries—customer service, retail, and hospitality.

Toshiba in 2015 introduced a humanoid robot, Aiko Chihira, for interacting with customers in Japanese. Dressed in a kimono and smiling, Chihira greets shoppers at the entrance to Tokyo's Mit-sukoshi department store.

## Connected healthcare—the Internet of care

Connected healthcare is an uber term that covers digital health, eHealth, mHealth, telecare, tele-health, and telemedicine. Using digital technology to improve caregiving and patient experience by enabling communication between patients and caregivers is becoming more prevalent in the United States and across the globe.

For example, in its more remote areas, Africa is underserved by institutional healthcare. People can use smartphones to monitor vital signs and receive clinical advice remotely, ensuring quality treatment and saving people the long trek to the nearest healthcare facility. In Alaska, telemedicine is the key to providing health coverage in relatively inaccessible remote areas.

ReWalk would enable people with spinal cord in-juries to walk again. Yitzi Kempinski, uMoove's founder, says that several neurological diseases can be diagnosed by reading eye movements. uMoove plans to turn mobile devices, laptops, and even video game consoles into diagnostic devices.

In the United Kingdom, clinics monitor patients' sleep, exercise, diet, weight, blood pressure, and blood-glucose levels, and use real-time video con-sultations with patients. And in Australia, a digital monitor manages the health, wealth, and nutrition of the Australian Rugby team players to ensure their top performance.

Emerging technologies for remote care are increasing the demand for home care. The healthcare delivery model is changing with connected smartphones, sensors, wearable devices, networked devices, and services.

SudaMed Co. Ltd, a medical devices company, founded by Mazin Khalil, revolutionized healthcare in its native Sudan and Ethiopia, Kenya, Lebanon, and Jordan. It is dedicated to providing the first comprehensive digital patient record system that can run across an entire country without necessarily having access to the Internet or smartphones. SudaMed has grown rapidly and now has a history of 60,000,000 patients, changing how healthcare is tackled in the region.

Mobilheatlthnews, mHealth, telehealth, and social media will combine to evolve into the new healthcare delivery model; wearables and embedded sensors will move into the mainstream. There will be a shift toward preventive care solutions that offer early detection, behavior modification, and increased patient engagement.

## Virtual reality, real association
How we educate, train, and assist workers in completing difficult tasks in economies that need frequent reskilling is redefined by virtual reality. For example, virtual and augmented reality devices simulate training sessions to upgrade worker

skills to perform more demanding tasks. During the COVID-19 lockdown, Norwegian oil rigs were maintained by Italian engineers using virtual reality because the engineers could not fly. Virtual Reality Media, a Slovakian company, specializes in state-of-the-art simulators and training systems to train students in virtual scenarios. It demonstrates simulated normal, abnormal, and emergency procedures as they apply to the operation of aircraft. Given the critical need for re-skilling in the future, this represents an enabling capability.

GE is building a simulation engine, called the Digital Twin, that creates a digital replica of every significant technology system that GE makes: every jet engine, locomotive, gas turbine, MRI machine, and others. Each Digital Twin is an image of systems in the physical world. The Digital Twin of a jet engine would incorporate information from its design and the provenance of its supplies, and store data on its operations' locations and conditions. The Digital Twin is useful because it can predict when an individual component is likely to fail or when it needs to be replaced before it happens, saving lost money and time with repairs and outages.

## Sharing economy–collaborative consumption

A peer-to-peer collaborative consumption structure brings some additional income to owners and can be cost-effective and convenient for consumers. The same consumers can also become the owners at the same time. The platform makes it easier to aggregate supply and demand. Smartphones with navigation apps can find an affordable hotel room nearby or the best price for a rental car. Companies in the sharing economy space have just a skeletal corporate hierarchy that supports them. For example, Airbnb's corporate staff runs the Internet infrastructure for the apartment rental marketplace, and Uber's runs the web application that allows drivers and passengers to connect through their smartphones. Such peer networks are robust networks with no hierarchy in the system whatsoever.

A new set of problems has surfaced. How do we coordinate and align these networked teams? How do we get them to share information and work together? How do we motivate people in the absence of traditional reward systems? How do we encourage people in a company with a flat hierarchy that no longer promotes "upward mobility" and "power by position" in leadership? The network of teams rewards people for their contribution, not their "position." The days of "positional leadership" are going away, to be replaced by growth and career progression based on an employee's skills, alignment with values, followership, and contribution to the company.

In the book *Team of Teams*, General Stanley McChrystal describes how this structure helped the US Army during the war in Iraq. He had to dismantle the functional structure in place, build these teams, empower team leaders to take charge, and build a digital information center to help these teams co-ordinate.

Millennials, currently more than 50 percent of the workforce (more in many countries), are looking for a culture of missions and values at work. When they work in small teams, they need a shared culture to ensure that strategies, programs, and compliance consistently occur. Millennials do not aspire to mimic the styles of older senior leaders.

## 3D printing—small is agile

3D printing, still far from mainstream, is poised to revolutionize the world according to the Institute for Ethics and Emerging Technologies (IEET) study "Seven Emerging Technologies That Will Change the World Forever." Traditional manufacturing in-volved metal cutting, machining, and welding. A product can be designed on a computer and "printed" on a 3D printer, which creates a solid ob-ject by forming metals, plastics, and other mater-ials and shaping them into desired outcomes. A 3D printer can make many things that are too complex for a traditional factory to handle.

Compared to traditional manufacturing and proto-typing methods, 3D printing offers the potential for high degrees of customization, reduced costs for in-tricate designs, and lower overhead costs for short-run parts and products. These printers may be able to make almost anything, anywhere.

If the supply chain mechanism is disrupted, there can be a solution. For example, a remote construction worker needs a specific tool but can no longer have it delivered from the nearest city. He can download the design and print it, avoiding the delays caused by some parts' shortage. Additionally, he can avoid making upfront planning and investments for storing inventory for these products.

The applications of 3D printing can range from toys to high-tech customized parts of military jets. Today, 3D printers can print clothing, circuit boards, furniture, homes, and even chocolate. A company called BigRep can create an entire table, chair, or coffee table in one print. Fashion designers such as Iris van Herpen, Bryan Oknyansky, Francis Bitonti, Madeline Gannon, and Daniel Widrig lead the 3D printed fashion movement. Divergent Microfactories (DM) prints a 3D printed high-performance car called the Blade. 3D printing is also already used for architecture, aerospace engineering, medicine, industrial design, civil engineering, fashion, and food.

RepRap is a 3D printer that self-replicates. At Cornell, engineers have 3D printed human ears, and 3D printed prosthetics meet a heavy demand in the developing world. 3D printed organs are poised to revolutionize transplants of various kinds. As Gary Scott, a futurist, asks, "What happens when 3D printers print 3D printers?"

## Maker Movement

When you give people the means of production, it changes the world. The Maker Movement puts the power in people's hands to fund, design, manufacture, and sell their goods. This shift in production also shifts power from large, capital-intensive enterprises to individual producers. According to Forecasts, 3D printing is set to accelerate the maker movement. According to the Maker Movement study, the movement has already started with 135 million makers in America comprising 18 million small businesses in the US and accounting for two out of every three new jobs.

## The Energy Internet

in his book, The Zero Marginal Cost Society, Jeremy Rifkin describes the Third Industrial Revolution platform as three Internets (Communication, Energy, and Logistics) converging to operate as one. He sees the IoT bringing these three elements together to manage (Communications), power (Energy), and move (Logistics) economic activity.

The energy Internet is a perfect example of a collaborative economy. Some elements of energy internet, according to Rifkin, are a) transforming buildings into micro-power plants to collect renewable energies on-site, b) deploying storage technologies to store intermittent supplies of power, and c) using Internet technology to transform the power grid into an energy Internet.

The renewable power users will be electric plug-in and fuel cell vehicles that can buy and sell green electricity on a smart, continental, and interactive power grid.

## Money 2.0—the buried open source treasure

The future of money will be a wide range of choices for methods of transactions. As proposed by Nobel Prize-winning economist F. A. von Hayek in The *Denationalisation of Money*, a free market of competing currencies will become a reality. There will be many ways to pay for products and services other than cash, credit cards, and digital wallets. Blockchains will reinvent money. It endeavors to produce better and stable forms of money than a government does.

Money 2.0 is a world in which smart contracts (conduct of credible transactions without third parties) and side chains, two derivatives of the blockchain, can create currencies that solve social problems and streamline business as never before.

Most well-known cryptocurrencies, Bitcoin, Litecoin, and Ethereum, operate on a decentralized basis and use cryptography for security and anti-counterfeiting measures.

Stablecoins are tied to a specific asset, such as the US dollar or other national currencies. Tether is one of the most promising stablecoins, now ranked high among the most valuable cryptocurrency. It can also be asset-backed coins tied to commodities, such as gold. Examples include USD Coin, Gemini Dollar, and TrustToken.

Consortium stablecoins are issued by groups rather than by individual organizations. Libra was supposed to be backed by financial assets such as a basket of currencies and US Treasury securities to avoid volatility. Stablecoins also enables instant cross-border payments.

## Nanotechnology

A nanometer is one-billionth of a meter. Materials' characteristics, such as their color, strength, conductivity, and reactivity, can differ substantially between the nanoscale and the macro. Carbon "nanotubes" are 100 times stronger than steel, but six times lighter.

Nanotechnology can increase energy consumption efficiency, solve intractable health problems, and increase production at reduced costs. Nanomaterials are already being used in pharmaceuticals, sunscreens, bacteria-killing socks, composite bicycle frames, water filtration gel, solar cells, chemicals, and catalysts.

## Logistics Internet—the worldwide physical web

All transportation sector inefficiencies, such as running semitrailer trucks almost half-full after every drop and often returning empty, provide an excellent logistics Internet opportunity.

Centralized management of warehouses and distribution centers is not the most effective way to transport products. Some products' seasonal nature means that there are periods during the year when warehouses are underused, while at other times, they are overextended. Most of these inefficiencies result from a dearth of common standards and protocols that would encourage greater collaboration and more efficient sharing of logistics resources.

So, people such as Rifkin are looking to the Internet to rethink how we do logistics on a national and global scale. As Rifkin explained, "A packet of information transmitted over the Internet contains information on both its identity and routing to its destination. The data packet is structured independently from the equipment, allowing the packet to be processed through different systems and networks, including copper wires, fiber-optic wires, routers, local-area networks, wide-area networks, etc."

Similarly, he hopes that firms could collaborate and share logistical resources to increase efficiencies and productivity and lower costs. His idea is to create a "logistics Internet" using sophisticated algorithms that would enable companies to store items and ship most efficiently at any given time.

He explains the potential impact: "We'll be able to have a transport system where we power vehicles from energy from our energy Internet, and we'll power our electric vehicles and fuel-cell cars, trucks, and buses powered by hydrogen, all of that from our energy Internet at near-zero marginal cost to transport it."

"This transport and logistics Internet is connecting with the energy Internet and the communication Internet, which provides the data in one system," he says. "It is a game-changer. It is one of the great technology revolutions in history."

# CHAPTER 3

## Digital transformation: the second coming of customization

Digital transformation brought us full circle from the pre-industrial age when cottage industries flourished and had intimate relationships with customers. The first and second industrial ages created distance between producers and consumers. Networks and digital communications have restored closer bonds with customers virtually, often on social platforms.

The first industrial age changed communities with the mechanization brought about by the steam engine. Cottage industries of the pre-industrial age had social bonds with their communities and understood their cultural mores, tastes, and preferences. Mechanization of the first industrial age uprooted communities and created distance between manufacturers and customers. Impersonal market forces mediated the interactions between people and producers, lacking the human touch typical of the pre-industrial age.

The second industrial age was the mass production

of standardized products, such as the automobile in the early 20th century, that further separated producers and consumers. Products were uniform and indifferent to the peculiarities of human tastes and preferences. Digital transformation brings back the pre-industrial age of humanity without sacrificing the industrial and mass production eras' economic benefits.

Flexible digital platforms create an environment in which customization does not necessarily come at a higher cost. You could imagine designing your clothes, shoes, or accessories, and getting them printed at a low price. We are not far from that era when the industry can step up to meet each customer's highly individualized needs.

## Direct brands—radically transparent

The direct-to-consumer trend in retail markets epitomizes the third industrial age, characterized by mass customization. It thrives on recognizing the pain of mass production and the pleasure customers experience from fulfilling their individual tastes. Putting customers center stage and cost-effectively building processes and tools to meet each customer's need has emerged as a profitable business proposition.

Exponential growth rates in direct brands stand out in stark contrast to otherwise stagnant retail markets. SiO tripled its revenue in 2018 compared to the meager 4.5 percent of the US's care and beauty market.

Direct brands' growth outpaces even e-commerce; Kylie Cosmetics garnered 420 million sales revenue in its first 18 months compared to the 24 percent growth of its e-commerce peers.

The popularity of direct brands is not uncommon; the US vitamin and supplement market grew by 7 percent in 2018, lower than the 13 percent growth of the e-commerce segment, while Goop, a direct brand, doubled its revenue.

Facebook makes it possible to make direct connections with customers; ninety percent of direct brands had a Facebook-dominant strategy for launch and rapid growth.

Pop-up stores are the way these brands build relationships with their customers. Barkbox, for example, opened the Barkpark in Nashville, which creates an ambiance of families relaxing while they shop for toys.

Canada-based Shopify has built a platform uniquely designed for direct brands to create online stores and conduct business quickly. Gymshark, an apparel company based in the UK, used the Shopify platform to build its pop-up store, set up POS terminals, establish a cash management system, coordinate communication on social media sites, and increase online sales.

Unlike Amazon, the Shopify platform is customizable for the needs of small merchants. It has an ecology of application developers who meet the needs of small merchants. In the decade ending 2018, Shopify paid out $100 million for the development of applications.

## New vistas for personalization
## —the *Star Trek* replicator

Personalization is expanding into new activities beyond consumer markets. Nanotechnologies are bringing personalization to medicine and diagnostics and 3D printing to manufacturing.

Nanotechnology targets treatment and diagnosis at the molecular level unique to each individual. By contrast, therapies aimed at organs, in the past, harmed healthy cells in proximity. Tiny nanoparticles, comparable to microscopic cells, bind at a molecular level for diagnosis and drug delivery, avoiding any impact on cells that are not diseased.

Nanotechnology makes point-of-care diagnostics possible, bringing great convenience in the COVID era when rapid testing is critical to prevent the virus's spread. People need frequent testing, which is not possible if they must visit labs.

3D printing is a departure from metal or plastic cutting that was characteristic of an earlier manufacturing era. Metal or plastic formation, or additive manufacturing, which fuses layers of metal created from powdered material, is the hallmark of 3D printing. Cutting slabs of metal leaves little latitude to shape products to meet the specific needs of customers. On the other hand, it is possible to mold the desired dimensions with metal forming for customized product manufacturing.

Early impacts of 3D printing are manifest in rapid prototyping. Manufacturers can shape and reshape prototypes precisely and quickly with 3D printing to accelerate the time to market.

Two professors at the Hebrew University of Jerusalem have developed a 3D printing platform for personalized food. It can print gluten-free, vegetarian, and vegan diets, and it can also print special diets using edible nano-cellulose fiber for those with special food requirements.

## A perfect storm, not in a teacup

The turbulence of disruptive change currently buffets economies, businesses, and societies. Platform-based businesses are upending deeply embedded modes of developing and commercializing technologies and serving customers.

According to a McKinsey research report, more than 30 percent of global economic activity—some $60 trillion—could be mediated by digital platforms in six years. The adoption rate among digital natives is markedly higher than incumbent companies that are attempting to catch up. While 43 percent of digital natives have launched a platform-centric strategy, this is true for only 23 percent of incumbents.

Amazon, Facebook, and Google are now heavily investing and developing AI and blockchain technologies to create Platform 2.0 models.

The digital-native platforms are turbocharging innovation with their corporate venture capital (CVC) arms investing in incubators and accelerators, in which the members of their ecology build new services and products. A survey by Boston Consulting Group found that incubator use among them increased from 59 percent in 2015 to 75 percent in 2018. Closer relationships with academic institutions have grown from 60 percent to 81 percent in the same period, and company partnerships from 65 percent to 83 percent. The platform companies bring their core strengths to accelerate the pace of innovation; Google with its forte in AI and Amazon in voice services.

These ecosystems benefit from partners' expertise from a growing number of industries; the BCG survey found that 83 percent of the ecologies around digital platforms had partners from four or more sectors and 53 percent from six or more. The participation of a greater diversity of industry partners contributes to the greater sophistication of products that operate autonomously, connected and remotely controlled, and use analytics to provide services.

For example, Google parses live feeds of parking lots and AI's status to create a list of nearby parking lots and garages available for occupation by vehicles in proximity. The Google Map application directs a user to the chosen lot. They also receive walking directions from the garage or lot to their intended destination. Soon, Google will also inform drivers about the inconvenience they may experience in using parking spots.

## Tour de platform—race to the top

The platform is an online marketplace to create a virtual business network that brings buyers and sellers together. In a platform ecosystem, a producer and user swap their roles. Platforms have the power to change entire industries and create new ones. Uber and Airbnb shook the transportation and hospitality industries. They did not have to make any investment in the hardware of their businesses. Instead, they created networks of communities that provided deployment resources in novel ways to serve customers.

Uber created a platform that pools the information on available rides at any location and the demand for them in real-time. Customers can get rides when they need them by communicating on mobile devices. In the old days, riders had to call a company that represented a subset of available taxis, such as yellow cabs, and wait for a considerable time if any were not immediately available.

Airbnb turned temporarily unoccupied residences into guest houses, lodges, or hotels. The travel industry greatly expanded as more people could afford to go on vacations. Airbnb built a platform for users to conveniently discover houses or apartments to rent or lease and to pay for them.

Networks are inherently destabilizing as they unleash centrifugal forces for propelling forward movement. They bring together masses of people who can frictionlessly interact with each other to create new experiences. The exchanges between them create new opportunities for revenue generation and social betterment.

Naspers, a South African company, was steeped in newspapers and pay-TV's legacy businesses, which were wilting because of the spread of digital communications. Taking a platform approach, it rose like a phoenix and achieved exponential global growth, which eventually led to listing its spinoff Prosus, one of the largest in Europe, on the Amsterdam stock exchange. Prosus is an investment platform for funding businesses in Naspers's core businesses—classified ads, payments, e-commerce, and delivery.

Naspers's businesses create a virtuous circle of growth as each feeds into another by completing the cycle of e-commerce transactions. Its payments business thrives in countries where credit cards and banking services are not widely available. Naspers's PayU makes it possible to transact payments by alternative means such as e-wallets, mobile transactions, or e-invoices. Letgo, its shopping application, lets users determine the value of their second-hand products by pointing their smartphones at them, making its classified ad business more attractive than competing services. Its e-commerce business in food is made attractive by adding a delivery service.

Tencent's WeChat, deemed as a super platform, has become a global phenomenon with its integration of messaging, payments, communications, and e-commerce that is popular even outside China. It realizes economies of scope by creating a single, convenient conduit for customers to access multiple services. It draws customers with ease-of-use of its interface, uses mini-apps that do not require downloads, eschews advertisements, and earns revenue from commissions on payments and transactions. Chinese travelers overseas can get a prepaid-SIM card, which saves them roaming charges and motivates them to remain with WeChat and use it as a single interface for transactions, bookings, and communication with their peers. As their usage increases, users earn rewards.

Networks' repercussions go far beyond a means to connect people. They have become touchpoints for customers for not only purchasing, but the entire customer journey. Depending on the touchpoint type, they indicate how customers become aware of products, revealing early intention to purchase when they compare products, narrow down their choices, and make decisions. Individual segments of customers will make their journey from alternative routes all captured from web stream data. A young couple searching for baby products for their first child will likely explore their options, while those expecting their second are more likely to compare and decide. Current marketing needs analytics to understand these journeys and provide relevant content to attract customers.

These networks have a far-reaching impact on societies. For example, Iranians from all walks of life organized a massive protest after an unprecedented Twitter storm, sharing the hashtag #DoNotExecute, protesting the judicial death sentences of three men arrested after nationwide protests. Five days after the campaign went viral, Iran's Supreme Court agreed with the retrial request.

Corporate organizations are more open to collaboration, free from hierarchies, to develop adjacent technologies for connected products. For example, connected homes are a composite service that includes camera monitoring of the elderly, remote control for lighting and heating, and more. Xiaomi's home platform brings together the individual services from multiple vendors and packages it as one service for the customer.

Amazon, another super-platform company, embeds its voice assistants in multiple industries and use cases. For example, it collaborates with Cerner in the healthcare industry to automate populating electronic health care records by entering the essential information it extracts from doctors' and patients' conversations. Amazon is also gaining traction in mobile voice commerce, especially for small merchants who sell customized products that elicit a disproportionate search for customers' information.

Social networks have recreated entire industries as communities on platforms interact in unexpected ways. The music industry was one of the first that experienced a cataclysm as iTunes became the platform for discovering new artists and distributing songs. Music labels are extinct now. Out of the old industry's ashes came the remarkable rise of indie music, which had a market share of 40% of the market in 2017. Star musicians still exist, but indies are a new cult in the music industry. Two thirds of social media users revealed that they discover their music on Facebook or Twitter. Music platforms such as Spotify create an environment for indie bands to gain exposure, interact with their fans, and distribute their music. Playlists on platforms spread the word about new artists.

Using social platforms, companies such as L'Oreal and Kiehl's cultivate community bonds through interactive and personalized experiences with customers that evolve as a company learns from listening to chatter on social media platforms and the views expressed on blogs and review sites. L'Oreal historically interacted with hair salons, and its local charities earned goodwill by contributing to community causes.

In the digital world, L'Oreal has relationships with a network of influencers and pop-up stores where it organizes unique events for clusters of customers. On the Tmall platform in China, L'Oreal had social influencers livestream to offline pop-up stores to greet customers and help them explore its brands. Customers have also been wowed by augmented reality experiences on Snapchat to virtually try new beauty and hair styling products.

Nike supported New York's inner-city basketball

courts as part of its brilliant "Sport Changes Everything" ad campaign to connect with underappreciated communities and empower girls as athletes. The reward, of course, was customer loyalty.

## 20 x 20 network effects

The networked economy is the convergence of people, platforms, and business. It's about all these elements connecting in real-time. The beauty of a platform is that as it grows, it develops "network effects," which means that it gets much more valuable as it expands. "Metcalfe's Law" says that a network's value is proportional to the square of the number of nodes in the network. For example, if a network has 20 nodes, its inherent value is 400 (20 × 20 = 400). Over time, network effects create entry barriers, and new entrants find it hard to compete with them.

Networks are not just a means for communities to connect; they are also a way to alter the game rules for business by addressing unserved social needs. As social groups reap value that significantly improves their quality of life, they are also more receptive to related services that transform entire industries. M-PESA, a mobile application provided by Safaricom in Kenya, was initially intended to offer microloans to communities unavailable from banks. Soon, it became a means to make money transfers among peers. It has provided a portfolio of financial services in recent years, including savings (in collaboration with banks) and merchant payments. The penetration of financial services in Kenya, as a result, rose from <u>75%</u> in 2016 to 83% in 2019.

IoT will extend networks' reach to every corner of the world and use the data for new services to automate daily activities and streamline workflows. It already has billions of devices and a wide variety of sensors, equipment, and wearable computers. Homeowners returning from their workplace on a cold day, for example, will be able to remotely turn on the heat from their smart cars before entering their home, and enjoy the comfort of a warm room.

5G will bring a step-change in the scale of IoT with massive machine-type communications— sensors embedded in every building, transportation network, hospital, sports stadium, city infrastructure, and factory. The volumes of data generated by the IoT will be so large that it will no longer be possible to process and analyze at a centralized location on the cloud. The IT infrastructure for big data analytics, the platforms, and application development will move closer to communities where people live, work, and play. There will be a greater need for partnerships for integrating communication, computing, and analytical processing to achieve solution design objectives. The old hierarchies of individual corporations will no longer be a viable means to benefit from emerging technologies.

Massive machine-type communications will spawn an entirely new generation of services. For example, hospitals will have better control over temperatures for refrigeration of their vaccines, cell cultures, and expensive medicines such as immune-therapy drugs. Germs are more likely to enter refrigerators when their internal temperatures are lower than the room's external temperature. It is currently hard to collect data at such a granular level and aggregate it in a processing database. Mesh networks connect with the last meter, interconnect with last-mile systems, and steer data flows to clouds.

Machines will be able to communicate with related devices to automate many functions. For example, connected cars will connect with parking garages and automatically make payments for parking without human intervention.

Communities will benefit from pervasive computing as situational and contextual awareness is heightened with data flowing to and from every corner. Today, public safety has to cope with devastating fires that spread rapidly in buildings with the human capacity to absorb information falling well short of needs. Similarly, terrorist attacks bring catastrophic destruction to downtown areas with numerous high-rise buildings in proximity to each other.

The IoT, at the edge, including sensors, cameras, and thermal imaging, will bring together information from all corners and display 360-degree views on wearable XReality glasses, enabling public safety workers to avoid dangerous hotspots. The glasses display a snapshot of the situation on augmented reality glasses with natural controls for executing actions. 5G communications makes it possible to reduce latencies to less than milliseconds and transport high-bandwidth video footage to speed up decision-making. Peer-to-peer communications built into devices can help rescue teams communicate and collaborate with their colleagues and partners with hands-free communications with voice, eye movements, and touch controls.

Tracking criminals is daunting in densely populated cities where there are many dark corners to hide in and elude the police. Today, infrared technologies help law enforcement see in the darkness and detect humans hiding by reading the differences between ambient and body temperatures. When police officers hear gunshots, they need to know where the shots came from. Today, sound-tracking sensors of tiny microphones and analytical processing capabilities embedded in devices help trace gunshots' origin, so the police don't waste time guessing and therefore arrive at a crime scene more quickly.

## Riding the wave

Digital transformation has a snowball effect, as integration and interaction of multiple technologies have a compounding impact on products and services and operating processes and systems to precipitate exponential change. Established businesses have little time before they can move to implement alternative business models.

Kodak, an iconic company in its heyday, fell by the

wayside with the emergence of the digital camera invented in its laboratory. Borders was dismissive of e-commerce in books but then found that people had little use for its brick-and-mortar stores.

The most recent impact of shifts in technology is Intel's floundering, while AMD has risen like a phoenix from what seemed like its ashes not so long ago. Nanotechnology has changed the rules of the game in the semiconductor industry. Manufacturing of nanochips takes forming processors from an atomic level while the old technologies, lithography, cut the material to shape the chips—the former is a more specialized process. AMD focuses on the design of its chips and outsources the manufacturing to Taiwan.

# CHAPTER 4

## Platforms and Networks

*"....ecosystems develop in virtuous cycles through network effects. By offering products and services that individual companies could not create on their own, ecosystems draw in more and more customers, which creates even more data, which allows artificial intelligence (AI) to fashion even better offerings, which in turn further improves processes and wins more customers."*
McKinsey: "Ecosystems 2.0 Climbing to the Next Level"

Multi-technology platforms and network technologies increasingly affect individual businesses and have broader impacts on industries, economies, societies, and communities. While technology platforms and networks are the nerve center of the technology universe, they generate services delivered on mobile and wearable devices to almost anyone. The Internet of Everything brings together intelligence from all spheres of work and life.

Automation diminished most technology plumbing, and users interact with technology with greater ease and with natural user interaction using speech, touch, gestures, eye movements, and (in the future) brain interfaces. IT resources are now available at our fingertips by way of graphical user interfaces on smartphone devices, laptops, and desktops, and servers as software reflections of hardware become available with virtualization. These graphical user interfaces bring visibility to information resources on individual devices, and entire networks spread worldwide.

The reach of the networks extends to communities in factories, educational institutions, and offices. Users do not necessarily have to be on-premises— they can access IT resources remotely on their mobile devices.

Travelling CXOs remain in touch with the workplace and execute their decisions remotely on 3D digital twins that help simulate and visualize alternative courses of action. Natural language processing and sentiment analysis keep them aware of the impacts of their decisions on employees and communities.

Situational awareness has expanded as the IoT brings information from otherwise invisible worlds. For example, sensors keep operations staff aware of wind speeds that affect renewable power generation in distant regions. Executives can make decisions on wind turbines' tilts to maintain power generation regardless of the wind direction.

New visualization tools help us to understand complex realities. Digital twins, for example, allow us to see manufacturing labyrinths from a single vantage point. We can simulate industrial processes on these digital twins to understand multiple scenarios in complex worlds.

More than ever before, we need our uniquely human attributes such as reasoning, imagination, and creativity to use technological tools to transform our world.

Digital transformation is the culmination of two decades of evolution of information technology that has lowered costs with expanded automation, sharply reduced manual effort, increased the speed of production cycles, and increased choice for a vast array of customer segments.

In the past, digitization was confined to devices and specific solutions. Desktop computers were hardware devices before the advent of Microsoft Windows, when a graphical user interface allowed users to execute functions with a mouse. After that, individual computer services were simply pieces of software that performed tasks with a mouse click.

A similar evolution is underway for infrastructure equipment such as servers, storage devices, and network equipment such as routers and switches. They have now been virtualized and show up as pieces of software on user interfaces that can be invoked and combined as needed to provide services such as driving an application. Cloud computing delivers the services on-demand, freeing companies from making risky fixed investments.

The cloud automates much of the human effort of IT staff. Hyperscale networks of large platform companies, such as Facebook and Google, span the world.

Cloud computing is now pivotal to driving business processes in business entities and communities. It is the storehouse of their information; the epicenter of intelligence, applications, and infrastructure resources; and a record of all their activities. They are now all visible on user interfaces and visualization software and accessible from mobile devices.

Digital transformation converts paper documents into digital files, paving the way to create vast repositories of data and information. Virtual functions replace hardware functions for remote control. Digitization automates processes that dovetail into the entire lifecycle of the daily activities of individuals. Communities interact more frequently because virtual communication is costless.

Additionally, data extraction from digital documents takes far less effort than reading them from paper documents and transferring the information to databases. Once extracted, the data can be aggregated and analyzed for decision-making. These decisions can be remotely executed, from the cloud, on processes in distant places, such as factories, to operate a collaborative robot.

Digital transformation marks a fundamental break in the trajectory of industry evolution and society as far-reaching as those of the steam engine, electricity, the automotive engine, and the Internet in the past. It prepares the ground for creating entirely new industries. The steam engine not only affected the manufacturing industry, but also used railways that brought about broader societal changes. Electricity gave rise to a host of industries such as washing machines, air-conditioning, and other consumer durables and relieved homemakers of the monotony of household work to be able to go out and work. The automotive engine mechanized agriculture with tractors and harvesters, and shifted farm workers to urban locations. Later, the Internet gave rise to application development such as social communities, which has increased interaction among people across geographies. Digital transformation has given rise to industries such as robotics, transportation-on-demand, and telehealth.

## Cloud computing and platforms

Today, virtualized networks and cloud computing bring together heterogeneous resources, across multiple clouds, for application development. And all entrepreneurs need is an interface to make use of these vast resources for innovation. A case in point is drones that inspect disaster zones—they have varying needs for bandwidth and other network resources on-demand. Mobile Virtual Network Operators (MVNO) assemble network resources to support them.

Platform-as-a-Service from the cloud brings together the toolsets that developers need to rapidly build new applications. Ideas matter more than the technical resources because their building blocks, microservices, have accumulated over time and can be pieced together to incrementally provide a stream of solutions. Unlike in the past, it is unnecessary to build monolithic applications each time users need to adapt to market needs. Hence, the risk, the investment, and the complexity of new product development have dropped markedly.

The cost of application development has declined as it is increasingly automated, aided by AI. New tools such as digital assistants help developers complete their code just as with e-mail messages in Gmail. Natural language AI reads through requirements documents to detect ambiguities and incomplete specifications, and correct them.

Platforms change the infrastructure of innovation and the human environment for the stimulation of creative ideas. In such an environment, a virtuous circle of creativity continuously generates new ideas as members of the ecologies are exposed to information streams, ideas, and content from their peers. Developers brainstorm on ideas in hackathons and use sites such as GitHub to collaborate in accelerating application development.

The coming together of platforms, data, and content and ecologies creates network effects that continuously expand the horizons for innovation. Apple was a small company when it entered the mobile devices business, compared to the market-dominating Nokia and BlackBerry. Apple crushed them entirely by changing the distribution model for music, which sold a song at a time from an app store. The ever-growing number of applications that developers hosted on its app store continuously created value that overwhelmed the incumbents.

Apple's market growth did not stop with retail customers. It spontaneously brought societal changes as Apple users used their devices and applications at their workplaces, especially outside their offices. It upended the culture of employees working on-site with equipment purchased by their employers. Anytime, anywhere work became commonplace. For example, salespeople started to spend more time with customers because they were relieved of the paperwork they had to do on-site.

## Platform 2.0 and network effects of intersecting technologies

The second generation of platform technologies is becoming the crucible in which multiple technologies such as AI, the IoT, and blockchains intersect to generate novel business models, products, and services and interact with communities in unforeseen ways.

## Platforms and AI

Artificial intelligence brings insights from large and heterogeneous datasets to learn about customer behavior and social interaction. Based on the insights gained, it is possible to increase engagement with customers on social communities. A richer understanding of the culture, quirks, and social mores of customers helps to customize products. Information services bundled with commodity products increases margins. Long tails of products make their discovery costly.

The Commonwealth Bank of Australia used its wealth of data on customer interactions on its platform to identify those who were most in distress due to the COVID pandemic and brought relief to them by the deferral of their repayments.

RBC builds relationships with car dealers, who are conduits for its loans to new buyers of automobiles, by sharing future business forecasts. The car dealers, in turn, can better manage their inventories.

Emotion detection is a new kind of AI from companies such as Affectiva, a new way to customize messages and services. Customers are more likely to be receptive to products and advertisements when they align with their moods.

Ant, the financial services arm of Alibaba, began its journey into financial services with AliPay, its mobile payment services, as an alternative in a society in which credit cards were absent. The bigger payoff for Alibaba was the data generated by the cash flows of individual customers. Its AI engines, hosted on the cloud, estimated the creditworthiness of customers for lending purposes.

Alibaba pivoted to qualifying prospects and recommending them to banks for loans when the regulatory authorities prohibited the loans' securitization without reserving capital for them. It has now expanded its financial services business into asset management and insurance. It serves as a *de facto* financial advisor by using its analytics tools to match financial services products with customers who need them most.

The strategic advantage of pooling large sets of datasets is encouraging the horizontal and vertical integration of industries to benefit from their information sources. Amazon, for example, has widened its business from books to an ever-increasing range of retail markets. Similarly, Apple is broadened its business into all mobile devices, whether handheld or wearables, and their applications.

By eliminating intermediaries, Amazon significantly lowers its distribution costs, which allows it to offer free shipping services and streaming content to its prime members. Due to low transaction costs, Amazon can provide a long tail of products, services, and streaming content from a wide variety of cultures and producers. By contrast, Hollywood thrives on occasional blockbusters. Apple has now focused on monitoring health and fitness, potentially creating a new market for preventive care services in the near-term future.

## Platforms and IoT

The IoT blends into people's daily routines to minimize friction in activities as they are still in process. Sensors read the signals in the environment and deliver services when they are needed.

Driving is one of the daily routines that are fraught with potential accidents, inattentive driving behavior leading to pedestrian deaths, and congestion caused by unguided traffic. Vehicle-to-vehicle communication mitigates the risk of collisions. Warnings to drivers about the dangers of their behavior can prevent accidents. Prompt redirection of traffic to less congested routes can prevent its slowdown. 5G brings comes with ultra-reliable low latency communications, which is fast enough to alert drivers in time to avoid accidents and possible deaths.

Increased personalization and customization of products is challenging for factory shopfloors as their lot sizes become smaller and smaller. Additionally, customers' tastes and preferences are fickle, and machines need to be reconfigured to adapt. Orders flow unevenly as the fortunes of customer segments of customers wax and wane with the economy's fluctuations.

Collaborative robots (cobots), armed with computer vision and reinforcement learning algorithms and operating from clouds, help cope with fleeting demands for customized products. Optical sensors built into cameras help robots adapt to changing needs because they can read the parts' dimensions. Reinforcement learning algorithms can learn to ensure that the robot and the pieces fit.

## Platforms and blockchains

The security and trustworthiness of suppliers, products, and services have been a weak digital transformation link. The state of credit for global supply chains <u>illustrates the importance of trust</u>. Banks are risk-averse; their evaluation methods are labor- and paper-intensive. They are also unreliable in times of crisis, as was demonstrated in 2009 when exporters from emerging markets were the first to lose access to supply chain credit. While alternative sources from the capital markets exist, they need to trust many small suppliers from distant countries. Similarly, supply chains are rife with theft, insertion of counterfeit products, loss, and degradation of products in the absence of control over the environment.

IoT and blockchains play complementary roles in building trust and security in the supply chain. Sensors all along the supply chain automatically create a record of goods movement and check for environmental variables, such as temperature, and unauthorized entry into facilities, such as warehouses. Blockchains create a decentralized peer-to-peer method, rather than use a lengthy and costly process, to verify suppliers.

## Platforms and edge computing

Together with 5G networking, edge computing coalesces cloud computing and platforms into local activity flow and opens a new vista for application development. It inserts itself into cities, ports, factories, and farms and creates services for the minutiae of daily activity that bring order, convenience, and relief into segments of communities. It is possible to execute tasks that were too tedious, expensive, or logistically overwhelming to be viable in several cases.

Bridge inspection is one such activity that has long been neglected and eventually leads to bridge collapse and fatal accidents. It is challenging and dangerous for humans to reach underneath bridges or take measurements, capture imagery, and then analyze it. Drones can inspect bridges more frequently because they are remotely guided to sections of bridges to check for their stability.

Seaports and airports are the hubs of a medley of barely coordinated activities that teeter on the edge of chaos. At ocean ports, goods move from ships, barges, cranes, and trucks in multiple directions while winding their way through customs, inspections, and warehouses. In all these processes, there is a risk of congestion, misplacement, theft, and damage. Similarly, airports manage passengers and cargo flow to aircraft, all with the risk of delay, sabotage, and cargo or baggage misdirection. Edge computing platforms, aided by sensor data, are beginning to bring order and efficiency to people's and goods' movement.

Quality of life is an overriding consideration when people choose a city where they want to work and live. Commute time, crime, transportation, and leisure time activity choices are some of the influences on quality of life. Traffic congestion is a fact of life in most cities, but streamlining its flow between alternative routes affects commute time. Some people may be reluctant to use a toll road, but they would be willing to pay if they knew how much time they would otherwise spend in traffic. People can quickly find empty parking spots using information delivered on mobile devices instead of driving around to search for a space. Smart street-lights can redirect traffic with a change in the lights' color of a series of lamp posts, when traffic chokes up due to accidents, rallies, or natural disasters.

Edge platforms can be the focal point for aggregating the data from city repositories and citizens to mine for traffic patterns to anticipate choke points. They can be the hub where city problems and solutions are discussed and resolved. Developers can choose from several pools of data needed to craft new solutions.

## Platform and ecosystem

Digital platforms and their ecologies today are the most dynamic segments of the US economy. They are hiring legions of gig workers, tenuously controlled by remote mobile or computer applications. Managements' standard methods of exercising controls have attenuated; wage and salary incentives, promotions, cultivating cultures, human relations, and hierarchy are congruent with on-premise work inside firms, but not for masses of gig workers.

Platform-anchored gig work needs a new rule book that takes advantage of the flexibility, ease of knowledge and information sharing, and resource pooling that becomes possible with large platforms. They will have to find ways to complement the strengths of their platforms with the skills that other entities and individuals bring to it.

For relatively low-skilled functions such as driving for Uber, intermittent work opportunities for retired workers, single mothers or caregivers, and students are attractions that override the uncertainty of compensation. Such workers benefit from information sharing, such as expected earnings from time spent, which will help them make choices to increase their revenue. For example, drivers need information on the cost of reaching their clients to determine whether the compensation of the time spent to drive to a clients' destination is worthwhile.

For skilled workers, the value of platforms is in the clusters they create. They are sources of shared resources, such as tools, for individual categories of application development and shared knowledge, intellectual property, information, and content to encourage their growth. Developers are potential entrepreneurs, and platforms draw them in by opportunities to sell their applications through digital stores, preferably branded for their category.

Individual platforms have shared visions of the approach and methodologies for application development. For example, IBM has contributed to Hyperledger, a hybrid blockchain platform for public and private blockchains. While public block-chains bring the strength of security that protects against intrusions by intelligence and government agencies, private blockchains keep corporate information safe from unauthorized disclosures. Private blockchains are an anathema to those who believe in permissionless blockchains, and they are unlikely to join the IBM ecology.

# CHAPTER 5
## Succeed with shared
## mental models

*"You can't stop the waves, but you can learn to surf them."* – Hawaiian proverb

A high tide of turbulence makes it hard to see beyond the fog of uncertainty. Our ability to validate our decision choices to achieve our desired outcomes will determine our chances of achieving success despite the haze of the view ahead.

As we know, the term digital transformation tops the pantheon of overused buzzwords, right above agile transformation. The digital transformation is not merely an implementation of digital technologies but also about digital ways of working and interactions, transforming the way we do business. We can think of it as the application of new mental models to achieve the goals of transformation.

Digital transformation is a concept that is hard to define. Without a shared mental model, people will have their own distinct understanding of the word with different implications.

Amazon's 14 Leadership Principles is an excellent example of shared mental models used to make all big and small decisions. Without shared mental models, all company strategies will dissolve into a primal chaotic culture. Even if the company achieves success, it will be in pockets that optimize locally, but there will be almost no global optimization.

Another Seattle-based company operates on the principles of "Truth, Bit, and Pull." It tries to make almost everything (within permissible limits) transparent, such as employee salaries, expectations from work, and daily operations. There is no room for closed-door meetings, and all meetings are open meetings. The common denominator of its culture is small. It keeps its teams small, batch also sizes small, and similarly small releases, short meetings, and a faster feedback loop.

It creates a pull culture, self-help in essence, by allowing employees to volunteer in all activities. The workforce is encouraged to pull vital company communications, identified by QR codes, from a central location and pull work from other teams instead of waiting for the management's big push. Employees can pull their annual performance reviews and rewards instead of waiting for one large push at the end of the year.

The biggest drawback of not having mental models is that people view the same problem, opportunity, and risk through their own mental lens, likely colored by their past experiences. Without a shared mental model, people tend to operate without a shared understanding of the context. Mental models are critical in migrating people to growth mindsets that rely less on past experiences and more on knowledge acquired by an empirical process—build, test, and learn.

Successful enterprises have adopted new mental models to thrive in the new world. They have shifted their orientation and set themselves up to move quickly. That means a fundamental change in selecting and managing priorities, designing their solutions, and striving for outcomes.

I'll propose seven mental models that cover various facets of digital transformation to suggest how successful companies are surfing the high tide of change and thriving amazingly well.

## A shift from the right to left

Working backward from learning about customers to product design is as hard as trying to unlearn to ride a bicycle after learning to ride it. Bicycle riding becomes second nature after you have learned it—you do it without thinking about it. Destin Sandlin created a bicycle that moves in a direction opposite of the intended course, as unlikely as it may seem. He made the bicycle that would go left if you turn right and go right if you turn left. It took him eight months to learn to ride a bike in this contrarian manner.

The new economy needs you to think backward. Amazon, and many other companies, encourages working backward from the customer's point of view. It does not start by developing products but by immersion into the customer's realm. The experience imbues the processes of product development with customer empathy. You get into a customer's shoes. The converse of getting into the producer's shoes before doing it for customers is like trying to untie shoelaces while walking.

Working backward would mean an internal press release with announcements of customer needs and the means to fulfill them. It will spell out the customers' problems that need solutions. After the initial press release, the product manager edits it and reissues it several times in the subsequent few weeks to all the peers and stakeholders until they arrive at a promising conclusion.

A shift from left to right is not confined to working backward from the customer. Shift left also means not to test in the end, but test continuously using acceptance test-driven development. Shift left helps us focus on the real customer behavior first, which takes a great deal of conditioning of your mind. The development team picks up one core user scenario and starts writing the acceptance test before writing code to meet that test.

Most likely, you must have heard these common quotes:

"What gets measured gets done."

"Measure what matters most."

"If you measure it, you can manage it."

Shifting from right to left means first defining the

purpose of metrics before you collect the data. Data collection is a means to an end to create a report. Before you determine the metrics, it helps to ask this: what business problem it will solve? Then, you focus on how to collect data that tells the right story to justify that investment.

In this mental model, you keep the team outcome-focused. You define an outcome first, then create solutions to achieve them. It allows the entire team to stay focused, aligned, and committed to the real result, and effectively meets your goals. It takes a great deal of training, but backward planning leads to higher levels of success.

## Be data-driven—open your third eye

Why do you need this feature now?

What data points do you have to support this feature?

Why can't you wait till the last possible moment?

These are some of the questions people ask in a data-driven organization. They don't only comply with their seniors' gut feelings; instead, they decide objectively on the best available information.

They collect both structured and unstructured data that floods business every day. It gives businesses the third eye to understand their companies and convert the knowledge into action for a competitive advantage.

Most importantly, regardless of their position in the hierarchy, everyone in a data-driven company can access data and tools to test their ideas and hypothesis. Access to data empowers people, leading to rapid innovation.

The touchstone of Amazon's company culture is its reliance on metrics. Every activity is measured— web design, product, finance, HR, or operations. Decisions are based on the data collected, organized, tested, and made accessible to all. As a result, metrics inform the way Amazon operates its businesses. Nordstrom uses a personal information system called Personal Book for better customer service, such as sending a personal note on a customer's birthday or thanking a customer for a past purchase. Because Personal Book is confidential to the company, Nordstrom has various ways of using personal information to serve customers better.

Organizations use data to gain customers, improve customer service, validate the efficacy of their ideas, find new revenue opportunities, and reduce costs—it all depends on how creatively they want to tackle business challenges. As a result, the value of corporate data has increased exponentially, as well as the importance of data science.

In this mental model, the transformation is about learning ways to use data effectively, giving the right people access to data to make decisions quickly, and building data literacy to speak in terms of data.

## You fail to conquer success

When it comes to ideas, quantity rules over quality. The greatest artists and writers are prolific—

Picasso produced more than 50,000 works, and Vincent van Gogh 2,100. Mozart and Beethoven were the most prolific composers. Great products in the modern era require more experimentation. Gone are the days of market research. The more ideas you test out in the market, the more likely you will identify a concept that will rock the market.

An anecdote in David Bayles and Ted Orland's book *Art & Fear* explains the dangers of exploring a minimal number of options. "A ceramics teacher divided his new class into two groups, telling one group that they would be graded solely on the quantity of work produced, and the other on quality. On the last day of class, the first group's work would be weighed and graded accordingly. The second group would be graded on quality, however much or little work they produced. When grading time came, however, it turned out that the highest quality works all came from the group graded for quantity. While the quality group agonized over what would constitute first-class work, producing very little in the process, the quantity group went at it, emphasizing productivity – but also, being artists, always trying to improve."

Many companies are rethinking the way they do business. It may be one of Google's motivations for creating its Alphabet structure in 2015, splitting itself into smaller and more agile units. GE's FastWorks or Lockheed Martin's Skunk Works have been great examples of learning to fail fast in pursuit of achieving something big by creating a portfolio of unicorns within the enterprise.

Failures are integral to success—you win big when you overcome significant challenges. Failure does not chasten you; instead, you see it as a fork in the road that leads to a path to a solution. There must be eagerness for effective learning to solve the bugs in production (not deliberate though), versus having no bug. Systematic experimentation promotes learning. No one knows better than research scientists that failure is not optional in their work; it's part of mega-success at some stage.

By contrast, we are so obsessed with seeing the project's green status that we aim for 100 percent success in all our projects in corporations without leaving room for making course corrections should we run into a failure. Experimentation comes after the fact instead of a natural process of achieving goals. Inevitably, products are overdesigned to please everyone with all the features customers could seek but had not expressed a need for. Alternatively, they play it too safe and create an optimal product without being sure of what is needed. You don't need to try dramatic experiments with significant investments. Often, a small pilot, a dry run of a new technique, or a simulation is sufficient to get it right.

Digital transformation is about building that resilience, creating that culture of experimentation in all departments of the company to stand up and run relatively quickly, despite failures.

## Learn from your customers, learn it all

In traditional companies, a product manager orchestrates product development. He or she does the market research, combines it with the judgment of some of the highest paid people, their own experience, and the company's product vision, and one fine morning deliver the product to the customer, keeping their fingers crossed. The product managers know that product launches will either succeed or fail in the market.

In the digital world, we become humble. We do not claim to know our customers. We approach customers with a minimum testable product to gauge customer interest, tweak the product iteratively, gather feedback, and keep working with customers until we fulfill their needs. Customers are never a hundred percent satisfied, which makes them the source of innovation. We test the hypothesis with customers, do not rely on our gut feeling, and continue to deliver the products that delight customers.

Instead of relying on market research, many companies now prefer to perform experimentation such as A/B testing to build and test new products and services. Experiments help to learn when something cannot be deduced logically or predicted confidently.

Companies are using virtual environments to test out their ideas at a lower cost of failure. Proctor & Gamble uses a 3D virtual store to run faster and cheaper experiments than using real market tests. Vocalpoint and other online user communities help the company in the dry run.

The majority of P&G's initiatives are now using a virtual toolbox. To make supply chain improvements that add consumer value, they invest in "sense and respond" capabilities as part of a "consumer-driven supply network." That highlights inventory strategies such as continuous product replenishment, produce-to-demand manufacturing, and dynamic replenishment and distribution.

Google's "one percent rule" is legendary. This approach involves measuring results to reveal what is working and what needs further experimentation.

To adapt, a company must have its eyes and ears ready to read signals of change from the ecosystem, understand its implications, and react quickly to reshape the product or reinvent the business model. The UK-based grocery giant Tesco performs detailed analyses of the purchase patterns of the more than 13 million members of its loyalty-card program. Tesco reads shifts in customer behavioral patterns early and provides what customers exactly need in each store. The online storefront complements Tesco's business model and offers a broad range of products and services. Tesco also provides consulting services to others on its analytical capabilities.

Google famously uses algorithms to increase an ad's relevance to an individual search or the advertiser's bids on keywords. The relevance increases the click-through rate, which means more revenue for Google. By linking its advertising data directly to its operations, Google can make decisions in a split second.

The key to success in this mental model is adopting the growth mindset of being humble, accepting that we don't know much about customers' ever-changing needs. We learn from the customers by trying things out, collecting data, measuring impacts, and pivoting where it is appropriate.

**Listen to the story–stories make you link**

Words make you think, and stories make you see the links. Humans have been telling stories since 15,000 B.C. to connect, entertain, and pass along important information through generations. Now storytelling is coded in our genes, and storytelling is wired into human brains. When we tell a story, listeners try to get in tandem with the storyteller: the storyteller plants ideas, thoughts, and emotions in the listeners' minds.

Disney is one of those companies that is great at storytelling. Disney movies are not about Disney, they are about Mickey Mouse, but they connect very well with real life. Solving a real-life customer problem is very much in the vein of a Disney script. Product development is not about the product or the people who develop the product—it is about the customer. There is a hero, a problem, a failed attempt to solve the problem, plan B, revelation (an aha moment), last-minute glitches, and finally, overcoming the pain and transformation to reach a successful outcome.

To create a story around the customer, first you need to understand the customer. The narrative will differ from customer to customer. Then create a villain in your account, and the villain could be a low credit score, debt, poor shopping experience, taxes, and fines, or anything. Our goal should be to empathize with customers and equip them with the weapons (our products) to defeat that villain. The final part of the storytelling should have a happy ending, indicating success.

## Promote change and challenge

Inculcating a culture for innovation takes curating the elements to embed its DNA. Innovation is a group activity, a mindset of creativity, which creates an ambiance for creativity. Opportunities for innovation lurk in the challenges of day-to-day work, not in labs. Below are seven factors that instill a spirit of innovation.

Daily necessities and stresses are the mothers of continuous innovation. Grassroots workers experience the pressures of daily work and have the desire to overcome them. They could, for example, innovate when parts for old equipment are longer available from vendors. Networked organizations free them to innovate autonomously.

Hierarchies, by contrast, stifle people with processes. Yet, hierarchies afford the comfort of stability, predictability, and continuity. Using microservices as a metaphor, we should be able to package both in a container and not be constrained by a single operating platform. That will allow technology and business to progress together on a Wardley map. A separate track for innovation will kill it.

There is no shortage of people who wax eloquent about innovation; harping about innovation is a rite of passage, a cult in management. Agile is buzzing with terms such as Scrum, continuous integration, sprints, and time boxes, and hums incessantly. Making it a part of the daily rhythm of work/life is another matter. Innovation, embedded in our daily routine, feeds on itself; it invests people in advance of innovation, in a virtuous loop that scans for innovation possibilities, evaluates the outcomes, and suggests new ideas.

Some of the popular innovation techniques that companies adopt to curate innovation culture are as follows:

- **Analogy thinking:** It studies comparable products, solutions, and processes to learn about best practices in the same domain and transfers knowledge that sparks ideas to adapt methods for the environment of a similar company.
- **Barriers and boosters:** Innovation journeys can run into barriers that range from attitudes, organizational inertia, talent shortages, and more. Conversely, rewards and collaboration agreements with sources of knowledge boost them. A trained eye can spot the opportun-

ities to remove barriers and accelerate progress in innovation.

- **Brainwriting**: Brainstorming comes to mind when we want to bounce ideas and serendipitously generate a brainwave in a group. As with other group activities, brainstorming is swamped by the dominant extroverted personality in the room, sidestepping introverts. Brainwriting lets each person write down their ideas and present them to the group. Alternatively, they could iterate by discussing them around a table.

- **Co-creation:** It takes a bottom-up approach to new product and service development in which employees participate instead of following directions from senior managers. Their collective intelligence accelerates innovation. By contrast, a top-down approach misses employees' tacit knowledge, who can bring perspectives from multiple vantage points. They are also less likely to resist change when they are involved in initiating it.

- **Concept cards:** It summarizes a product or solution concept, listing critical ideas about the target audience, the needs served, and how it makes money.

- **Feedback grid**: It summarizes the information from user feedback, spelling out key points such as what works in a product, the desired outcomes, and possible pathways to achieving the desired attributes in products.

- **How might we statement:** It spells out how to frame a challenge and open it for discussion to find solutions and turn them into opportunities for growth.
- **Hybrid thinking:** It is used in settings of complex problem solving, it encourages multiple perspectives on the same problem and trains people to synthesize them.
- **Linear unpacking:** It structures fragmented information, separates the wheat from the chaff of stories, and spells out the logical upshots from them.
- **North Star:** It is an overarching vision that the senior most executives articulate and communicate that helps to marshall the expertise of the ninjas in the organization to deliver on the financial goals of companies.
- **Open innovation:** Large companies that operate in silos and hierarchies by forming smaller cross-departmental teams and new forms of working, such as hackathons.

- **Speed-storming:** It is about creating teams comprising members with compatible personalities who achieve high-speed performance by compounding their passions.

Transformation in this mental model is about trying new ways to get better results. Its implementation requires getting out of your comfort zone, being situationally aware, and using your creativity to find a new answer to an old problem. It requires exploring multiple solutions to the problem and disrupting others before being disrupted.

Wardley mapping has often been used in business to anticipate changes and create a roadmap. Using Wardley mapping business explores the most suitable reactions to change—or even pre-empt it—and highlights the supporting role of technology for inspiring a clear, competitive advantage. At the same time, mapping equips a business with advanced techniques for gaining that competitive environment to its advantage.

Wardley maps are about building a shared understanding of your context to provide the situational awareness necessary for building a sound strategy. All this is especially helpful if you start a business, create a product, inspect the competition, analyze industries for opportunities, or even anticipate what the future might hold. A Wardley map represents situational awareness, and it lists shared assumptions about a context and hints at what strategic options are available.

A Wardley map consists of a value chain or activities needed to fulfill user requirements graphed against evolution—how individual activities change over time under supply-and-demand competition.

In mapping, you take your value chain and plot the components along an evolution axis covering genesis, custom-built, product (+rental), and commodity (+utility). All the elements in the map evolve from left to right due to supply-and-demand competition. As they mature, they change from an uncertain, uncommon, and continuously morphing state to a more standard and commoditized stage. For example, a mobile phone is something commonplace and well understood. However, virtual reality is less common and less understood.

Using Wardley mapping, a leader anticipates the patterns of the forces that act on the environment, trains the organization in universally useful principles, and makes decisions that lead to victory.

## Balance the big picture with attention to details

Everyone wins if the system wins. Systems thinking is holistic; it derives an understanding of parts from the whole's behavior and properties, rather than the converse.

Systems thinking helps us explain the complex phenomena and interdependent issues that leaders face every day. Systems thinking means observing events or data to identify patterns and uncovering the hidden phenomenon. It is an awareness of the circular nature of the world that is our abode, an appreciation of the inexorable laws of systems that elude us, and a reminder that we cannot be oblivious to the consequences of our actions.

For systems thinking, it is critical to bring down the walls between departments or subsystems. The role of the systems thinking leader is to promote the wisdom of the system. Leaders must link their approach to other parts of the system, provide context at all levels, build lateral capacity through networks, and promote deep learning through collaborative problem-solving. It also requires harmonizing local optimization with global optimization and balancing local short-term and long-term goals.

This mental model sees the transformation as preparing organizations to deal with the current realities and get them future-ready. They learn to become uncomfortable and invest in new capabilities to tackle the future with an open mind.

One of the tools widely used to promote systems thing is the causal loop diagram. Causal loop diagrams are constructed by identifying the critical factors in a system and indicating the explanatory variables by visualizing them as links. By interlinking several loops, you can create a concise story about a particular problem or issue. Causal loops uncover deeply entrenched systemic problems.

First, you bring the problem to the table and engage

the team in some healthy discussion to resolve the selected issue. After a lively team-storming session, capture some crucial factors that are the problem's determinants; negative or positive effects on them precipitate a predicament. Your team may find many more factors, but incorporating too many elements will muddy the framing of issues.

You select a maximum of eight to twelve factors for optimal results using a prioritizing technique, such as dot-voting. Organize the selected items on a physical or digital whiteboard to be well scattered, preferably in a circular shape. Randomly choose one factor and see how that factor affects other elements on the board.

The facilitator invites team members to discuss relationships, asking the cause-and-effect relationship among factors. Is it because of (cause), therefore (effect)? If yes, how? Why?

The cause and effect would describe the relationship between the two factors. It could be in one direction, both directions, or there could be no relationship at all. Alternatively, you could choose to keep the relationship unidirectional by weighing in favor of a dominant factor. Repeat the exercise for all the elements on the board one by one until you reach the last factor and your mesh of relationships is ready.

Based on the calculation, you could see the dominant factors with a maximum number of ins and outs. This simple cause and effect modeling technique can help your team collectively build a shared understanding of your system at play.

## Understand each internal interaction through a customer's eyes

Customer journeys are arguably the most powerful mental model that incorporates the key elements of most of the other models by looking into each interaction through the eyes of a customer. A customer journey is a way to describe a series of interactions that starts with a customer need such as "I want to purchase a book," and it continues until the customer buys the book, or probably even after that.

Companies cannot effectively solve these needs until they work together. The marketing, IT, and operation or back offices work on these customer journeys together. It requires a vertical slicing of the organization, which runs at odds with traditional functional, hierarchical setup.

The companies that view these interactions through the eyes of a customer meet the need of the customer faster. Acquisition, retention, revenue earned, and repeat purchases affect business outcomes.

The Royal Bank of Scotland decided to adopt a new business model, after its meltdown during the 2007–2009 recession, centered around reducing the friction in customers' journeys to purchase homes. Now its teams collaborate so that its customers have to spend less time on credit-worthiness evaluations, home surveys, and the rest.

Deft steering of prospects across the customer journeys stimulates new product and services development that resonates with the audience and improves retention. Glossier a direct-to-consumer beauty brand, encourages conversations in its community in which customers contribute suggestions about novel products.

Technology platforms arm companies to acquire customers and retain them. These can be an array of context-specific information, such as geo-location, activity, and behavioral data. Technologies such as Foursquare reveal information to marketing professionals about people visiting shops; video analytics captures shoppers' window shopping and expressing sentiments about products. They post their commentary on social media. That provides an opportunity to serve messages and content at the moment to influence buying behavior. A shopper may find a new food product that interests them, but they will likely buy it to find recipes to help them cook it.

Analytics has created new possibilities for customer retention as human behavior is observed in real-time to identify the risk of customer churn. For example, the Royal Bank of Scotland contacts customers who are overdrawing on their accounts, and recommends financial advice to better manage their finances.

A painless experience of using products will reinforce the positive customer experience. A phone company will build goodwill when customers do not have to call it to inquire about delivery delays or understand how it functions and spend too much time setting up an account or disputing bills.

New technologies make it possible to remove much of the friction. Online purchases of clothing have lagged in other product segments. Apparel does not often fit well with the physical attributes of buyers. Similarly, furniture is hard to buy online because it may not align with individual homes' interior dimensions. Augmented reality is a way for shoppers to try, virtually, multiple options before selecting the one they like most. IKEA has an application that allows on-site shoppers to view furniture in their homes' virtual settings on a mobile phone before purchasing the items they want most. Sellers can save on the cost of returns by offering such an application.

A customer journey is not just a powerful tool to acquire customers, it is a means to transform the way we work. Customer journeys enable new ways of working to drive transformation and shape our thinking to deliver the product the customer needs. The change is not about recreating the legacy systems, or responding to the past problems. It is about getting a business ready for the future.

The journey cuts across siloed organizations and creates that socio-technical experience that promotes an agile mindset with cutting-edge technology. A systematic approach is needed to define a strategy and find suitable platforms to implement it.

The customer journey approach takes you deeper than visual maps. It opens the discussion about broader system changes by adapting to new culture, structure, practices, and ways of working at scale. In the absence of systemic changes, the journey will fail miserably.

Customers are placed right at the center of software development when its flow mirrors customer journeys. Agile teams can easily visualize and label customer interactions, prompted by their needs, in their development pathway. When organizations take cues from a customer journey, they are inclined to be outward-looking. The siloed front, middle, and back offices realize the importance of working together to solve customer problems. This approach challenges the traditional order designed for internal efficiency, but not necessarily for overall effectiveness, as is true in far too many companies.

Customer journeys inform development teams about customer expectations and prepare a coherent map to solve customer problems. A concrete plan meets customer needs by simultaneously pursuing development and positive customer experiences. A single-minded focus on the engineering strategy for growth and modernization can take attention away from ensuring that customer experiences are satisfactory. So, employees, leadership teams, and businesses need to invest in sufficient efforts to achieve company objectives for customer satisfaction.

The ideal way to implement the journey is to execute the entire value chain end-to-end right from kickoff. A project needs to create a skeleton plan, contact the customer for demo and feedback, and iterate the entire journey or mini journey together. This approach works best when a team or a collection of groups is empowered to work together, write the tests first, and include the customer early in the development process. A top-down approach geared toward internal efficiency does not jell with a customer-first method.

It is equally important to measure success with the right metrics. Many companies ask for the wrong metrics when they launch customer journey programs. They focus on velocity, or earned value, rather than outcomes of each journey or mini journey. The journey must have a direct connection between customer outcome and financial goals. If they are not connected, there will be a lot left open to interpretation, thereby creating a wide gap between customer journey metrics and overall purpose.

A customer journey includes functional and non-functional features such as compliance, legal, security, performance, accessibility, and risk. It should be a part of the considerations of the team that shepherds the passage from the start. Any function that has a meaningful role in shaping the customer experience should have a role in the development effort, even if it is indirectly involved.

One key to all the customer journey efforts' success is that they need to recur for them to take deep roots. It takes a village to implement a customer journey, and all those learnings are lost if the teams are not enduring. Lasting teams can experiment with new technology and improved ways of working together instead of finding new opportunities.

## Pitfalls to avoid

In all those exercises, it is easy to get enamored by the myriad of possibilities. The best is the enemy of the better. Do not get trapped into an infinite loop of options to come up with the best scenarios. Always start simple and stay focused on two or three significant possibilities. Those possibilities will open the door for new opportunities.

Be humble; it matters a lot. Don't ever assume that you have the silver bullet, and build your strategy around it. Creativity is not about finalizing the best option for the future, but rather about intelligently weeding out the scenarios that will not work.

When developing your hypothesis, try not to be myopic, focusing on the current situation, products, competitors, and market. The future is emerging very quickly; anticipate what the market and competitors' landscape would look like in the next few years and respond swiftly to it.

If you are in a sweet spot, raking in profits, do not allow complacency to sneak in. Always act like a startup and maintain the agility to respond as a startup would. Be frugal, as a startup should be; scarce resources also drive innovation and creativity.

# REFERENCES

Jacques Bughin, T. C. (2019). *The right digital-platform strategy.* McKinsey.

Ali Ghaheri, S. S. (2015). The Applications of Genetic Algorithms in Medicine. *Oman Medical Journal.*

Allison Mooney, B. J. (2015, May). I-want-to-buy moments: How mobile has reshaped the purchase journey. *Think with Google.*

Alspach, K. (2020, March 5). 5 Partners On The Biggest Opportunities With Microsoft In 2020. *CRN.*

Anna, P. C. (2018, March–April). HR Goes Agile. *Harvard Business Review.*

Annabel Fenwick Elliott. (2017, November 15). The first ever A380 superjumbo has gone into storage – so will it end up on the scrap heap? *The Telegraph.*

Banerjee, F. S. (2018, June 12). Enhancing Customer Insights with Public Location Data. *Harvard Business Review.*

Baruch, S. (2019, April 1). The Future of the Central Office. *ICT Solutions and Education.*

Becker, K. (2018, July 16). Trek now lets you build your bike, right down to the paint job. *Digital*

*Trends.*

Boudet, B. G. (2019). *The future of personalization—and how to get ready for it.* McKinsey.

Bradley Fox, M. a. (2020, August 18). Telehealth: Fad or the Future.

Bumb, D. S. (2020, January 22). AI is helping to make better software. *Deloitte Insights.*

Choudhury, P. (. (2020, November–December). Our Work-from-Anywhere Future. *Harvard Business Review.*

Cole, S. (2019). *The impact of technology and social media on the music industry.* EConsultancy.

COLVIN, G. (2020, August 10). The hidden—but very real—cost of working from home. *Fortune.*

Cooper, P. W. (2015). *Sharing or paring?* Price Waterhouse Cooper.

Economist. (2020). *What Ant Group's IPO says about the future of finance.* London: Economist.

Eyers, J. (2020, June 29). CommBank using AI to help triage loan deferral customers. *Financial Review.*

Fitch, A. (2020, October 28). AMD, Nvidia Chip Away at Intel's Semiconductor Dominance. *Wall Street Journal.*

Francois-Xavier Delenclos, A. R. (2018). *To Get Smart, Ports Go Digital.* Boston: Boston Consulting Group.

Gewirtz, D. (2020, August 20). First look: MakerBot takes 3D printing to the cloud with Cloud-Print. *Zdnet.*

Ghelber, A. (2020, September 30). How Smart

Brands Are Analyzing Offline/Online Reviews to Optimize Their E-Commerce Presence, Part 1. *Total Retail*.

Goldsmith, B. (2019). Digital Biosensing by Foundry-Fabricated Graphene Sensors. *Scientific Reports, Nature*, 1-10.

Guttman, C. (2019). Drone Innovation Turns to Edge Computing.

Holt, D. (2016, March). Branding in the Age of Social Media. *Harvard Business Review*.

IAB. (2019). *How To Build a 21st Century Brand Report*. IAB.

Jacobides, M. G. (2019, November 19). The Delicate Balance of Making an Ecosystem Strategy Work. *Harvard Business Review*.

Jacobs, B. A. (2012, March 27). Where Have I Seen You Before? *New York Times*.

Jethanandani, K. (2018, April 16). 5G network apps orchestrate human-robot collaboration in manufacturing. *FuturistLens Magazine*.

Jethanandani, K. (2018, July 31). Orchestrating competition with interfaces on virtual networks. *FuturistLens*.

Jethanandani, K. (2018, July 31). Upstarts harvest digital services on heterogeneous virtual networks. *FuturistLens Magazine*.

Jethanandani, K. (2020, October 7). Viable Uses for Nanotechnology: The Future Has Arrived. *Techopedia*.

Jose Maria Barrero, N. B. (2020). *Why Working From Home Will Stick*. Chicago: Becker Friedman,

University of Chicago.

Kahn, M. (2017, March 23). Old Fourth Ward dog park meets beer garden sniffs autumn opening. *Atlanta Curbed.*

Keldsen, D. (2011, December 20). Collaborative Innovation on the Retail Floor at Nordstrom's. *Innovation Management.*

Koning, R. (2020). *Digital Experimentation and Startup.* Harvard Business School.

Kripalani, N. (2020, March 3). Will Microservices become the mega trend of the decade? *ETCIO.*

Kubs. (2018, November 13). 3D Printed Sneakers and Mass Customization – Is Adidas There Yet? *Student Assignment, Harvard Business School.*

L'Oréal unveils latest digital innovation beauty. (2014, May 19). *Chain Store Age.*

Landi, H. (2020, September 16). Cerner senior exec: Amazon cloud partnership is driving Cerner's shift to become digital platform company. *Fierce Healthcare.*

Lang, N. (2019). *Key moments from World Economic Forum Annual Meeting.* WeForum.

Liao, R. (2020, January 12). China Roundup: WeChat's new focus on monetization. *Techcrunch.*

Listek, V. (2020, November 12). Formnext Connect: Nexa3D and Castor Announce New 3D Printing Material and Software. *3D Print.*

Marshall W. Van Alstyne, G. G. (2016, April). Pipelines, Platforms, and the New Rules of Strategy. *Harvard Business Review.*

Martin Reeves, K. W. (2019, April 2). Companies Need to Prepare for the Next Economic Downturn. *Harvard Business Review*.

McKinsey. (2011). *IT growth and global change:A conversation with Ray Kurzweil.* McKinsey.

McKinsey. (2018). *Winning in digital ecosystems.* McKinsey.

McLellan, |. (2020, Feb 3). Connected cars: How 5G and IoT will affect the auto industry. *ZDNet*.

McWaters, R. J. (2018). *The New Physics of Financial Services.* Zurich: World Economic Forum.

Michael Ringel, R. B. (2019). *How Collaborative Platforms and Ecosystems Are Changing Innovation.* Boston: Boston Consulting Group.

Michael Ringel, R. B. (2019). *Innovation in 2019.* Boston Consulting Group.

Muchmore, S. (2020, April 24). COVID-19 bill with $25B for lab testing signed into law. *MedTechDive*.

Navid Rabiee, M. B. (2020, July 20). Point-of-Use Rapid Detection of SARS-CoV-2: Nanotechnology-Enabled Solutions for the COVID-19 Pandemic. *International Journal of Molecular Science*.

Neslen, A. (2015, July 10). Wind power generates 140% of Denmark's electricity demand. *Guardian*.

Nicolas Maechler, K. N. (2016). *From touchpoints to journeys: Seeing the world as customers do.* McKinsey.

Noel T Southall, c. a. (2019). *The use or generation*

*of biomedical data and existing medicines to dis-cover and establish new treatments for patients with rare diseases – recommendations of the IR-DiRC Data Mining and Repurposing Task Force.* Orphanet Journal of Rare Disease.

Norris, M. (2020, July 24). Nestlé Accelerates Use of Augmented Reality Amidst COVID-19. *Packaging World.*

Omar Rodríguez-Vilá, S. B. (2020). Is Your Marketing Organization Ready for What's Next? *Harvard Business Review.*

Pathak, S. (2018, September 24). Network effect: How Shopify is the platform powering the DTC brand revolution. *DigiDay.*

Patra, J. K. (2018, September 19). Nano based drug delivery systems: recent developments and future prospects. *Journal of NanoBiotechnology.*

Payments. (2020, August 5). Alexa, What's The Future Of Voice Commerce? *Payments.*

Piscini, E. (2017). *When two chains combine.* Deloitte.

R, D. J. (2020, March). Innovation In Handheld Space Disrupts The Ultrasound Landscape. *Medical Buyer.*

Reuters. (2029). *M-Pesa has completely changed Kenyans' access to financial services, this is how....* CNBCAfrica.

Richard Dobbs, J. M. (2015). *The four global forces breaking all the trends.* McKinsey Global Institute.

Roma, H. S. (2020). *Breaking the Bank: RBS Remakes*

*Retail Operations Around Customer Loyalty.* Bain and Company.

Roush, W. (May 6th, 2020). *Podcast: How to break America's covid-19 testing bottleneck.* MIT Technology Review.

Schonfeld, E. (2008, March 27). For Chinese IM Portal Tencent, The Money Is In Micro-Transactions. *Techcrunch.*

Schulze, E. (2019, September 11). A $100 billion tech company you've never heard of just listed in Europe. *CNBC.*

Singer, D. C. (2015). Competing on Customer Journeys. *Harvard Business Review.*

Statt, N. (2020, May 25). 3D Printers are on the front lines of the Covid 19 pandemic. *The Verge.*

THIRUVENGADAM, M. (2020). *Inventors are eyeing your home office.* Chicago: Chicago Booth Review.

Thomas, L. (2017, Feb 27). From mass production to mass personalization. *Megatrends.*

Tice, C. (2014, October 30). Why Ronald McDonald Failed On Twitter: Branding Lessons. *Forbes.*

Unnikrishnan, M. (2019, June 27). The Biggest Airline Innovation of This Century. *Skift.*

Venkat Atluri, M. D. (2017, July 12). Competing in a world of sectors without borders. *McKinsey Quarterly.*

Victor Chang, P. B. (2020, June 21). How Blockchain can impact financial services—The overview, challenges and recommendations from expert interviewees. *Technological Forecasting and Soial Change.*

Violet Chung, M. D. (2020). *Ecosystem 2.0: Climbing to the next level.* McKinsey.

Voorveld, H. A. (2018). Engagement with Social Media and Social Media Advertising: The Differentiating Role of Platform Type. *Journal of Advertising*, 38-54.

Wexler, A. (2018, October 25). The African Media Giant That Wants to Create the New Craigslist. *Wall Street Journal.*

Wired. (2001, March 1). Founding Father. *Wired.*

# About the author

Ashok P Singh is a technology leader and a coach with over 20 years of experience in helping companies with agile transformation, innovation, customer journeys, and product management. He worked in leadership positions at Sprint, Microsoft, ATT, CapitalOne, Starbucks and several other companies. He advises many companies on business agility and transformation strategy based on the knowledgebase built incrementally by experimenting across the breadth of enterprise. Ashok is an active speaker and blogger on agility and transformation.